DIVIDEND GROWTH INVESTING

INVESTING

A Step-by-Step Guide to Building a
Dividend Portfolio for Early
Retirement

By Joey Thompson

damages, or monetary loss due to the information herein, either directly or indirectly.

Respective authors own all copyrights not held by the publisher.

The information herein is offered for informational purposes solely, and is universal as so. The presentation of the information is without contract or any type of guarantee assurance.

The trademarks that are used are without any consent, and the publication of the trademark is without permission or backing by the trademark owner. All trademarks and brands within this book are for clarifying purposes only and are the owned by the owners themselves, not affiliated with this document.

Table of Contents

Introduction vi

Chapter 1 - How Dividend Investment Works? 1

What Is A Dividend? 1

History Of Dividend Investment 1

Types Of Dividends 2

When Are Dividend Stocks Distributed? 6

Dividend Reinvestment Plan (Drip) 11

Why Do Companies Increase Dividend? 15

Factors That Influence Dividend Payout For Companies 17

Chapter 2 - Choosing Your High Performing Dividend Stocks 26

Dividend Aristocrats 26

Reits 54

To Conclude 63

Chapter 3 - Strategies And Pros And Cons 65

Pros And Cons Of Dividend Investing 65

Some Pitfalls And Risks Associated With Dividend Growth Investing 71

Strategies For Successful Investing 73

Chapter 4 - Should You Buy Reits? 75

Outperformance- Reasons 75

Benefits Of Reits 78

Disadvantages Of Investing In Reits 80

Types Of Reit Investments 82

Chapter 5 - Building Your Early Retirement Portfolio 86

Factors To Consider 87

Dividend Payout Ratio (Dpr) 93

How To Interpret The Dpr 94

Strategies For Investing Based On Dividend Yields 96

Chapter 6 - Tax Benefits From Dividend Investing............ 111

What Are Qualified Dividends? 111

Chapter 7 - Building A Stellar Portfolio...............................116

Why You Shouldn't Just Randomly Invest In Different
Companies... 117

Reasons For Investing In Dividend Stock Portfolio.............. 119

Selecting The Dividend Investment Strategy 132

Chapter 8 - Safe Portfolio Withdrawal.................................139

The 4% Rule 140

Reasons For Dividend Withdrawal.. 140

Chapter 9 - Understanding The Dividend Calendar 144

Chapter 10 - Six Commandments Of Dividend Investing...146

Dividend's Worst Year 153

Chapter 11 - Case Studies- Building A Successful Portfolio 155

Conclusion 163

INTRODUCTION

Any individual looking to invest some cash in stable returns must have heard of dividend investing and the opportunities that it offers. We all want to follow the footsteps of the likes of Bill Gates and Warren Buffet and earn a stable monthly passive income. Perhaps not as much, but only a fraction of what their ROIs look like would be great to have!

But here's the truth - those passive incomes did not come from passive decisions. There is a reason why most investors are avid readers - they learn before they apply. And you need to do the same. In order to yield stable returns, you need to know the ins and outs of investing in dividends.

No matter what professional stage you are at, it is always important to have an idea about various investment options before you put your money on the line. Many investors don't begin their research regarding investments until they are about to reach retirement. Retirement, however, is the ideal time to REAP the benefits of those investments, not the ideal time to make them. Does it mean that you can't generate a stable income post-retirement? Of course not! It just means the sooner you begin, the higher your returns will be in the long run.

Dividend investing is more than just a pastime and is often considered a stream of passive income with little to no effort required. Sure, that will come too, but before you can get to that point, you need to know the inside outs of dividend investments. You need to know exactly what companies to invest in and when. You need to be able to read tables and understand the influence of the economic and political conditions of a country that influence the market rates. Not to say you need to ditch your work and spend all your time reading books and watching newspapers. But just one rightly put together report, like this book, can help you make smarter and profitable investment decisions with dividends.

The purpose of developing an ebook for dividend investment growth was to serve as a guide for new and existing investors that have a particular interest in receiving regular income. I will begin with a brief explanation of the term dividend, expanding onto its types, important terms and procedures involved in it, and eventually, provide guidance to build an effective dividend portfolio.

CHAPTER 1

HOW DIVIDEND INVESTMENT WORKS?

What is a Dividend?

A dividend is a return on shares that a company pays its shareholders from its corporate earnings. Any and every successful business requires consistent cash flow to thrive. When investors buy shares of a company, they receive dividends or returns on the investment. Investors, also known as shareholders, invest in the hope of generating consistent returns in the future.

History of Dividend Investment

The emergence of dividend policy dates back to the 13th century when a French bank Société des Moulins du Bazacle offered dividends to its shareholders. Continuing to the 17th century, Dutch East India Company (VOC) became the first public entity to offer a regular dividend payout. For nearly two decades, VOC

1

continued paying approximately 18% of its share values to the shareholders. Although the dividend payout options were still low up until the 18th century, more companies introduced the policies pertaining to the industrialization and business growth.

Types of Dividends

Most companies have a Board of Directors as well as external and internal share and stakeholders. These Share and stakeholders are one way or the other directly influenced by the economic performance of the company. These stake and shareholders hold a little chunk of the company, in the form of shares. And thus, they also receive a share of the profits; one method of receiving those profits is known as dividends.

Dividend distribution can happen in one of many forms. The following are the five different ways dividends are distributed among the shareholders.

Cash Dividend

A cash dividend is when the company decides to pay back a small percentage of its earnings to its stakeholders in the form of cash. By making a cash dividend, the company's share price takes a dip. The price drop is often equal to the amount of the dividend.

Example

For instance, a company offers a cash dividend equal to 6% of its stock price. When the investor or stakeholder cashes out this profit, the stock price too drops by 6%. This drop is caused by the economic value transfer.

Stock Dividend

This is a suitable strategy for investors looking to invest long term. With this strategy, the company reinvests the dividends earned back into buying more stocks for the shareholders. Usually companies opt for this when they are short of cash flow or would like to hold on to the profits for further investment.

Property Dividend

Property dividends are paid in the form of assets, unlike the other two options that pay off in the form of cash or stock. Property dividend distributions are recorded at the fair market value of the 'property' or assets that are distributed. Fair market values are not the same as the book value of the asset and because of this slight difference, the company has the liberty to record that little variance as either a loss or gain, so as to alter their reported and taxable incomes.

Example

The company XYZ decides to issue special 500 identical signed prints by Pablo Picasso, which the company has kept stored in its vault for some years. The prints were acquired by the company for $500,000 and as of the date of dividend declaration, they happen to have a fair market value of $4,000,000. XYZ records the following entry as of the declaration date to record the change in the value of assets along with the liability to pay the dividends.

	Debit	Credit
Long-term investments-artwork	3,500,000	
Gain on appreciation of artwork		3,500,000
Retained Earnings	4,000,000	
Dividends Payable		4,000,000

On the date of dividend payment, XYZ records the following entry to record the payment transaction

	Debit	Credit
Dividends Payable	4,000,000	
Long-term investments-artwork		4,000,000

Scrip Dividend

It is possible that a company may not have the sufficient resources or funds to issue dividends in the near future. Therefore, it issues a scrip dividend, which is basically a promissory note (may or may not include interest) to pay shareholders at a later date. This dividend creates a note payable.

Example

XYZ international declares a scrip dividend of $250,000 to its shareholders at 10% interest rate. At the date of the dividend declaration, it records the following entry:

	Debit	Credit
Retained Earnings	250,000	
Notes Payable		250,000

Since the date of payment is one year later, XYZ has accrued an interest expense of $25,000 on notes payable. On the date of payment (assuming there is no previous or prior accrual of interest expense), the following entry is recorded by XYZ:

	Debit	Credit
Notes Payable	250,000	
Interest Expense	25,000	
Cash		275,000

Liquidating Dividend

This happens when the company decides to return the invested capital back to their shareholders. This often happens when the company is about to shut down and thus wants to return the investments. Calculations and process for liquidating dividends are similar to those of cash dividends, with the only difference that the funds are considered to come from the additional paid-in capital account.

When are Dividend Stocks Distributed?

Dividend dates are important to keep track of because they are a source of regular income. In understanding the process and distribution of dividends, it is important for the investor to know about the important dates including the declaration date, record date, ex-dividend date and the payment date.

The following section mentions and explains various important terms related to dividend earning. In order to understand the process, you need to understand these important terminologies.

Declaration Date

Every company selects a date for the dividend payout which is known as the declaration date. Details such as the record and payment date, size of dividend and other relevant details are provided in the declaration statement and are released along with the payment. Declaration date is also known as announcement date.

Example

Company XYZ declared dividend of $0.258 per size of dividend on June 15, 2019, and therefore it is recorded as the declaration date. This is different from the payment and record date which will be explained in the next section. The decision of the declaration date is taken by the board of directors and is disseminated to all the relevant shareholders.

Record Date

Also known as the cut-off or book closure date, the record date is the specific day when the company decides to pay the dividends to its shareholders. People often confuse it with the ex-dividend date and the easiest way to remember the difference is by understanding that ex-dividend date is set by the stock exchange and record

DIVIDEND GROWTH INVESTING

date is set by the company and the former occurs prior to the record date.

The shareholders for a company are not constant. New shareholders keep adding up as well as opting out and therefore it is important to ascertain the list of shareholders on a specific date. This also helps to eliminate the shareholders that have opted out so that the funds are appropriately distributed.

The record date is also important because it has a special relationship with the ex-dividend date. It is thereby important to understand that the record date may slightly differ between various stock exchanges such as the New York Stock Exchange and London Stock Exchange. In order for you to be in the record books, it is important to buy the stock at least 2 working days prior to their record date. This is because when the investor purchases stock from the exchange, it takes a while to update the details of the investor on the company's books. Normally the settlement period is based on the formula of T+2 which means that it takes two business days for the stock trading to settle.

For John to receive the dividend from the company XYZ on the record date, it is important that he should buy the stocks at least two business days before the record date or the ex-dividend date that occurs a day before the date of record.

The Ex- Dividend Date

One of the most important dates to consider is the ex-dividend date. It refers to exactly a day before the dividend record date and the first day when trade of stocks takes place without dividend. This date is set by the stock exchange where the trading takes place and the company has no role in setting the ex-dividend date.

Its calculation is based on the T + 2 system of settlement prevalent in North America which takes 2 business days to settle the stock trades after the transaction is completed. In case the investor buys the stock one working day before the record date, the stock trade settlement will take place in one working day after the record date. Therefore, the investor will not receive the dividend for that particular month. There are, however, exceptions to this rule. For example, if the value of dividend is more than 25% or above then the payment may take longer to process, but that hardly ever happens.

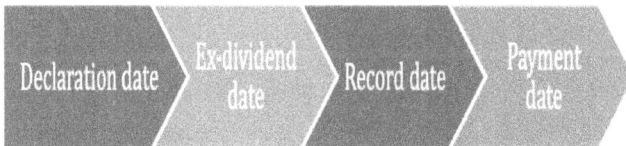

Dividend Yield

Not every company has a payout dividend policy. Therefore, the annual payout is the percentage of return which the company pays in relation to the share price. The dividend yield is taken as a positive key indicator of a company's growth because only the successful companies share their earnings. A simple formula to calculate the dividend yield is by dividing the annual dividend per share with the current price of the stock. The resulting amount is presented as a percentage.

Dividend yield= (Annual dividend/Stock price) * 100

Example

The company XYZ page out an annual dividend of $ 5.89 and its current stock price is $ 25.00. Applying the relevant formula, the company's dividend yield would be:

Dividend yield= (Annual $1.44/$53 * 100= 2.7 percent

It must be noted that the stock dividend yield is not constant due to the fluctuations in the market. Also, it is paid only when the company decides to do so.

Payment Date

As the name implies, the payment date is the date when the shareholders receive the dividend. There are various ways in which shareholders receive the dividend payments, including electronic transfer to the shareholder's account or a cheque being directly mailed to the investor. Companies around the world have different payment schedules. The US companies pay four times a year, whereas other international companies pay once or twice a year.

Dividend Reinvestment Plan (DRIP)

This term refers to the reinvestment of dividends into additional shares and is done automatically. This is useful in situations where the shareholders receive a small number of dividends. For the investor considering selling the stock with DRIP, it is important to consider the ex-dividend dates because the inability to do so will generate residual shares that the seller may not be looking forward to.

For instance, John purchases 50 shares of the company XYZ at a price of $23. This yields a dividend of $0.47 per share on a quarterly basis. If the stocks do not have a DRIP policy, the amount will be insufficient to buy stocks in the case of the DRIP plan; the dividend amount will then be reinvested to buy further stocks.

DRIP has a few advantages, such as the entire income generated from the dividend can be reinvested, and there is no commission to be paid. The stockholder must get the complete information of DRIP from the broker so that they are able to receive the advantage without any delay.

Accelerated Dividend

The amount of dividend paid before any changes in the dividend policy is known as an accelerated dividend. For instance, if there is a change in the tax rate of dividends, the company will release the payment earlier so that the changes do not affect the shareholders in a negative manner.

Example

For instance, the UK Treasury introduced a new tax policy on dividends on April 6, 2016. The policy entailed that the first payout of £ 5000 as dividend income will not be taxed. However, if this amount exceeded, the shareholder was liable to pay 7.5% of tax. Similarly, the taxpayer was supposed to pay 32.5% and 38.1% to be paid by the additional rate taxpayer. The marginal rate tax for the shareholders was increased to approximately 6% under this policy. In case that the company considered paying the accelerated dividend before April 6, the shareholders would be saved from paying a fraction of the liable taxes.

Special Dividend

Also known as the extra dividend, the special dividend is the amount that a company pays to its shareholders apart from the regular income distributed as per the dividend policy. This payment is non-reoccurring and is paid only once. The amount paid under a special dividend policy is greater than the regular dividend income. The shareholder receives this in case the company yields higher profits than it initially expected, or there have been other specific circumstances, like a special payoff, resulting in higher yield for the investors.

When a company has an excess of cash available on its balance sheet, and it does not plan to reinvest that cash in the business, the company may distribute the amount among its shareholders as a special dividend. For instance, Microsoft paid a special dividend of $3 per share in 2004. It was a onetime offering with the total value of the payout of $32 billion.

The company may also use a special dividend to further strengthen the bond of trust and loyalty with its customers. These complimentary offerings help gain the trust and loyalty of the shareholders. The ultimate purpose of investing in the stock is for you to have a source of regular income. Therefore, additional cash is always welcome by the shareholder. Think of it as a bonus but with the exception that there is no additional work involved.

If the company plans to alter its financial structure, it can release a special dividend by reducing the assets and equity of the company. As the special dividend is paid out, the company successfully alters the percentage of equity and percentage of the debt.

The cyclical companies often adopt the hybrid dividend policy in which a special dividend is paid along with the regular dividend since the companies are significantly affected by the changing economic situation.

The special dividend is paid only if the company has earned better profits and it is safer to adopt this policy rather than changing the dividend rate because in case of economic slowdown or recession, the company may have to decrease the dividend percentage and it often does not settle well with the shareholders.

Trade Date

It is a date when you purchase the stock by paying the complete amount. Trade dates play an important role in how taxes are collected. Taxes are usually calculated based on trade dates.

Settlement Date

It is the date that is decided between the buyer and seller for sale and purchase. Most commonly, it takes three working days for the stocks to settle after the trade has been carried out, and the seller and buyer have to share the stocks and make a payment, respectively, within those three working days.

Why Do Companies Increase Dividend?

When companies have a surplus amount of profit, they can distribute or invest those profits in multiple ways, dividends being one of those options. The decision, however, comes from the board of directors, and options are explored, keeping in view various factors. The following section lists various options for the company to consider.

If the value of company stocks is good, the company may repurchase them back from the investors. This reduces the percentage of shares floating in public, but doing so can be risky if the company fails to make anticipated profits in the long run.

Companies may look into paying off their debt by using profit through stock trade. This can help in the reduction of interest payments for the company.

Companies may also look into sharing profits with investors in terms of dividends. This decision, however, depends upon the type of management. If it desires to share its profits, it can do so in terms of dividends payout. The company can reinvest its earnings to develop further and enhance the company's growth.

This increase in dividends benefits both the company and the shareholders. The company is able to retain its shareholders while the investor is able to make stable and consistent growth in their profits. At the end of the investment, the initial amount of investment remains the same, while returns gradually increase.

There are two ways for an investor to make money with stock investments. The first method is where the stock prices take an immediate hike. Say an investor purchases 100 stocks at the price of $35 for each stock; say the price increases to $60 per stock in just 24 months. This means that there has been an unrealized capital gain. If the investor sells the stocks at the end of those two years, he is likely to realize again.

The other way is to get returns through dividends, and therefore the investor is likely to become an owner of a small portion of the company's corporate earnings. Dividends are decided by the board of directors and are most commonly paid quarterly.

An Example

Consider the well-known company Microsoft that did not adopt a dividend payment policy until its business gained momentum. The process took several decades to develop, and currently, it offers one of the highest paying dividends among other technological companies. The stocks have also witnessed unprecedented growth over the period of time, and investors have established trust in the company's performance.

Dividends are corporate earnings of a company which it distributes to the shareholders. The companies, however, are under no obligation to do the same. Companies like Google and Facebook do not have a dividend payout policy, whereas relatively younger companies prefer to reinvest their earnings. The companies that are more established tend to have dividend policies.

Factors that Influence Dividend Payout for Companies

There are well-established companies that do not prefer to share their corporate earnings with the shareholders because they find much more value in reinvesting for the growth of the business. Also, there may be a preference for avoiding the high cost associated with issuing new stocks and rather reinvest the earnings.

Increased Profits

When a company has a surplus profit, it may look into investing in further growth opportunities, making acquisitions, buying back its own shares, or debt payment. On the other hand, companies having less, or medium-scale earnings may not offer shares. There is a possibility that the companies making huge earnings want to share their profits with the investors.

For instance, the retired workforce has a particular interest in dividend policies since it offers a steady and lucrative stream of passive income. However, even for the investors, there are drawbacks of receiving dividends, the fact that they are taxable being one of the more significant ones.

Established companies that pay out dividends depict a prosperous and performance-oriented futuristic approach. It sends out a strong signal to the public that it is financially strong and willing to share its earnings with the people. A gesture of goodwill is created as well as the investors maintaining a trust level and loyalty towards such companies. Dow Jones, Verizon, Wells Fargo, and Eon Mobil are some of the companies that have successfully rolled out their dividend policies and have a strong investor build up.

Financial Discipline for the Company

Dividend policy may prevent a company from misallocating its capital. It also drives managers to work harder for the company. The investors expect higher yields in the form of dividend payouts. A dividend manager is in charge of creating sustainable and profitable cash flow for the investors and the company.

Paying out dividends helps keep the company's finances in control. A company may end up reinvesting the profits in less lucrative opportunities and thus fail to create healthy cash flow. Timely payment of dividends allows the company to offer consistent returns on the investments shareholders have made with them while creating financial discipline within.

Separation of Power

Another reason to have a dividend policy is to create a barrier between ownership and management. Dividends are proof that a company is into sustainable income growth. The board of directors is usually responsible for determining the payout ratio that needs to be shared with investors.

Aversion of Market Risks

It is a known fact that the value of dividends tends to grow with time. Companies that have been running successfully for many years have higher-yielding payouts compared to newer companies. Such companies have been in the business for more than 25 years and are often known as the dividend aristocrats. With shares in possession of investors, the company may also be able to buy them back in case of an economic recession. However, it is important to understand that investing in dividends does not guarantee consistent returns. There may be times when markets will fluctuate, and so will the payouts.

Financially strong companies pay dividends on a regular basis and keep on increasing the number of cash payouts in order to keep up with inflation. This is similar to receiving a hike in salary or increasing rent from your tenants in case you have a property rented out. It is, therefore, better to go with such stable companies so that the investors do not feel the pinch of inflation and continue to receive better returns.

Ability to Attract Investors

Dividends are essential in attracting investors. Companies offer dividends so as to lure investors in to invest in their business. Investors looking for ways to invest their money in a passive, yet stable stream will find dividend investments an ideal opportunity, most commonly to secure their retirement plans.

Companies require hefty amounts to set up, operate, and smoothly run a large business. Having that cash flow enables them to collect cash and then payout when the company is able to yield returns on those investments.

Searching for an Effective Dividend Policy

While choosing the stocks, many investors look at the current yield instead of the total return value. This may result in overlooking the balance sheet of the company, along with the potential consistency of learning the payout ratio. Therefore, it is important that in order to select the right company to invest in, its history must be thoroughly checked to ensure that the company has been paying a dividend on a regular basis. This reduces the risk of investing in a company that has a history of reduction in dividend returns or even elimination. The investor must consider a few characteristics while selecting the company to invest in by looking at its deliverables, especially during the economic slowdown. The following section lists the qualities that an investor must look at while building the dividend portfolio.

Having a keen eye on the changing economic landscape and business opportunities is a good way to start. A lot of online sources provide a diverse range of information that can be overwhelming and confusing, to say the least. This section covers everything you need to know before screening companies for dividend investments. Please note that these are general guidelines and cannot truly determine the credibility or the effectiveness of a company to offer desirable returns. However, thorough research will help you make informed decisions in this regard.

Greater Annual Growth Rate

The annual growth of the dividend must be greater than the current rate of inflation. Ideally, the dividend growth ratio must be prioritized against the average dividend offering. Knowing that the annual growth rate is higher than the inflation rate ensures that your investments will remain profitable and will increase in value over time.

There are exceptions to this rule. Say the annual inflation rate is at 4%, and the company is offering a stable 12% return. But the returns will remain consistent for the next three years. At first glance, it would seem as if the growth rate is not increasing each year, but in reality, the results would be better than a dividend return of 4% the same year with an annual growth of 2%. In this case, though, the investor would yield the same amount of returns for the next three years, but the overall profits would be much higher than a company offering increasing growth rates at a lower rate.

Needless to say, there aren't a one shoe fits all model of investment; whether you plan on becoming an active or passive investor, you will actively need to study each candidate company thoroughly.

Continuous Dividend Growth

The dividend portfolio must include companies that have at least 5% of dividend growth over a period of 10 years because that shows that the company is financially strong and will be able to give comparatively better payouts even during an economic slowdown. The best way to analyze that is to consider the performance of the company during the reception and expansion period. Avoid investing in new companies even if they show a strong alliance with well-established companies because such investments can be riskier.

Low Volatility

The stocks have a volatility rate in comparison to the market. This is known as the Beta rate, and it describes the risk ratio of the relevant stocks. It is important to consider that the stocks have a rather stable position in the market. Those stocks that significantly fluctuate possess a higher risk. The market consists of 1.0 beta and provides a scale of ranking for the stocks in the market. Those about 1.0 are riskier but can yield higher returns. The low beta stocks possess low yields as well as having a lower risk factor.

Learning how to measure beta is important for an investor. The basic formula for calculating beta is Beta=Variance/Covariance, and this is done by incorporating aggression analysis.

It is of utmost importance to analyze the volatility level of the stocks so that the risks are analyzed before making a purchasing decision. Of course, trust your knowledge and experience as well in establishing a clear decision but keep the beta ratio in mind as well.

All these terminologies may seem overwhelming initially. But once you get the hang of it, you'll be talking and walking the investor lingo in no time! Another word of caution: beta analysis of a particular stock does not depict the future returns and therefore, must not be considered as a final analysis because of other factors that influence the market, such as the index, inflation, and economic stability.

A few examples of the companies with a low beta ratio include AT&T with 0.56 and Colgate Palmolive with a 0.43 beta rate. These are well established and economically sound companies that have been in the market for decades and have gone through fluctuations and survived. As a new investor, it may be difficult to assess the volatility ratios correctly. As a rule, just make sure that the volatility ratio of stocks must be less than 1.0 in order for you to even consider investing with them.

Risk Assessment

An interesting tip to consider from the father of value investing, Benjamin Graham, is that while looking for stable stocks to invest in, one must look out for the margin of safety, a term that is used to differentiate the companies that have stood against economic fluctuations or instabilities. In doing so, the investor must look at the balance sheet of the company as well as the dividend growth ratio over a period of time. Make sure that there is no instance of overpaying because that can mean a high-risk level associated with stocks.

Don't Put All the Eggs in One Basket

It may become overwhelming while one is on a look-out for effective dividend payout policies. People tend to rush and invest as much as they can in a certain company's stocks, but that may not be the most suitable solution. At any given period of time, certain economic conditions and activities may slow down the growth of a specific company or even an entire industry or sector, whereas; the same economic conditions may become favorable for other industries.

In a situation like this, an investor with a diversified portfolio is able to sail through those fluctuating conditions without being affected. So unless you haven't promised your loyalties and your money to a specific company or industry (don't you ever!), you'd be better off having a diversified portfolio.

A quick look at investment portfolios of the top 10 or 10,000 investors even would help you understand the importance of diversification. Also, make sure that you don't just invest in different companies operating in the same sector, diversify in terms of industries too. For instance, if the price of crude oil increases by 20% overnight, then the entire transportation industry would be negatively affected, not just a specific airline. Hence, selecting multiple industries (more on that later) would help you create a stable and economically proof portfolio.

CHAPTER 2

CHOOSING YOUR HIGH
PERFORMING DIVIDEND STOCKS

Dividend Aristocrats

The dividend aristocrats consist of the 50 companies that have shown a significant increase in their dividend payout for the past 25 years. There is a certain criterion that the stocks must fulfill in order to become part of this list and must also be listed at the S&P 500. If an investor is looking for performance, consistency, and predictability, then this index is the go-to-place. Mostly, the dividend aristocrats are the blue-chip companies and have been committed to a steady and consistent dividend payout growth over many decades.

The criteria that a company must meet in order to become part of the list include the following:

- The company must show a dividend payout growth of at least 25 consecutive years.

- The company's stocks must be listed on the S&P 500.

- The company must have a certain market cap and fulfill certain liquidity requirements.

The aristocrat companies are good investment options because the stocks under this umbrella are mostly defensive and can sail through their difficult economic situations. One of the main reasons these companies are a viable option is because they have been able to build credibility and thus would always have a steady stream of income coming in from trusting investors, helping them stay afloat. Another important factor is that their dividends have been increasing for the past 25 years, giving them a competitive advantage over other companies.

As an investor, you must understand that these companies are not recession-proof. However, their performance and cash flow have not been significantly affected by an economic slowdown. For example, during the 2008 recession, the aristocrat companies had a decline of 22%, whereas the S&P 500 accounted for a loss of 38%. Hence, as an investor, it is a safer bet to invest in these companies since they have outperformed over the past few decades and adjusted their returns after facing the market risks.

Falling Out of the Aristocrat Index

This index is maintained by Standard and Poor (S&P) company, and it keeps adjusting the criteria every year in January. The companies that make up the index have to maintain their position and are added and taken off the index as per their situation.

How to Invest in the Aristocrat Index

There are many websites that provide the list of aristocrat companies and provides the required information to the investors to help them with their decision making. These websites have a number of criteria for the investors to select from. These websites offer valuable information regarding a company's position on the aristocrat index and how often it has fluctuated. You want to look for a company that has been able to retain its position over different economic conditions for it to be a viable option.

These companies are always under pressure with respect to their performance, and they often buy back their stocks in case of an outperformance. However, for the investors looking for a consistent income stream as well as dividend growth, the aristocrat index is worth referring to.

A common perception is that dividend-paying stocks always outperform the non-dividend-paying stocks because:

- This gives out the message that the company is shareholder-friendly since it rewards them in the form of cash payments.

- These companies take a lot of consideration while spending on the growth projects because they are issuing some of their earnings to the shareholders, and therefore such companies cannot afford to make any risky decisions. In other words, the capital allocation of the search company is already highly scrutinized.

- The companies that pay a dividend to the shareholder are likely going to focus on business growth so they can generate cash earnings in order to reward the shareholders, and therefore the riskiest stocks are already excluded.

The most recent analysis shows that sector-wise the consumer staples and industrials topped the aristocrat index. Next in line is the information technology sector that has significantly paved its way up to the list.

Company	Dividend Yield	Annual Payout	Payout Ratio	3-Year Dividend Growth	P/E Ratio
3M	3.56%	$5.76	60.06%	7.01%	20.74

A. O. Smith	2.21%	$0.96	38.71%	0.00%	19.44
Abbott Laboratories	1.62%	$1.44	39.89%	10.75%	43.06
AbbVie	5.79%	$4.72	49.95%	22.62%	37.59
AFLAC	2.04%	$1.08	24.27%	7.47%	13.05
Air Products & Chemicals	1.93%	$4.64	49.15%	6.88%	28.22
Archer Daniels Midland	3.07%	$1.40	N/A	0.00%	21.62
AT&T	5.57%	$2.08	57.78%	2.00%	16.73
Automatic Data Processing	2.09%	$3.64	59.00%	0.00%	32.00
Becton Dickinson and	1.13%	$3.16	25.12%	2.43%	71.96
Brown-Forman	1.02%	$0.70	N/A	0.00%	38.67
Cardinal Health	3.62%	$1.92	38.17%	1.58%	-3.77
Caterpillar	3.05%	$4.12	38.61%	9.95%	12.82
Chevron	4.29%	$4.76	68.10%	3.29%	15.93
Chubb	1.96%	$3.00	27.15%	2.08%	19.45
Cincinnati Financial	2.11%	$2.24	55.58%	0.00%	19.17
Cintas	0.91%	$2.55	33.55%	0.00%	33.09

Clorox	2.72%	$4.24	68.94%	8.93%	24.69
Colgate-Palmolive	2.48%	$1.72	57.53%	2.65%	25.71
Consolidated Edison	3.14%	$2.96	65.49%	3.50%	22.27
Dover	1.65%	$1.96	31.11%	2.50%	26.74
Ecolab	0.95%	$1.88	28.88%	0.00%	38.09
Emerson Electric	2.72%	$2.00	54.95%	1.28%	19.79
Exxon Mobil	5.40%	$3.48	100.58%	4.38%	18.73
Federal Realty Investment Trust	3.36%	$4.20	120.69%	0.00%	37.04
Franklin Resources	4.17%	$1.08	42.19%	9.17%	11.01
General Dynamics	2.25%	$4.08	31.70%	0.00%	15.69
Genuine Parts	3.17%	$3.05	51.69%	4.15%	17.67
Hormel Foods	1.94%	$0.93	53.14%	11.00%	26.61
Illinois Tool Works	2.43%	$4.28	53.77%	14.38%	23.21
Johnson & Johnson	2.54%	$3.80	41.71%	4.60%	22.10
Kimberly Clark	2.86%	$4.12	56.91%	2.02%	23.12
Leggett & Platt	3.26%	$1.60	62.50%	0.00%	22.12

Linde	N/A	N/A	0.00%	0.00%	N/A
Lowe's Companies	1.85%	$2.20	32.93%	13.12%	31.40
MCCORMICK & CO /SH	1.50%	$2.48	46.36%	0.00%	31.54
McDonald's	2.32%	$5.00	58.96%	9.29%	28.32
Medtronic	1.84%	$2.16	38.57%	0.00%	34.01
Nucor	3.34%	$1.61	40.97%	2.10%	11.64
Pentair	1.73%	$0.76	29.69%	N/A	20.78
People's United Financial	4.54%	$0.71	51.82%	1.08%	12.33
PepsiCo	2.67%	$3.82	64.09%	6.44%	16.37
PPG Industries	1.67%	$2.04	30.18%	6.27%	23.46
Procter & Gamble	2.38%	$2.98	59.60%	2.90%	74.20
Roper Technologies	0.53%	$2.05	15.11%	13.56%	35.32
S&P Global	0.77%	$2.28	21.86%	11.61%	35.40
Sherwin-Williams	0.80%	$4.52	18.59%	9.96%	38.00
Stanley Black & Decker	1.69%	$2.76	30.63%	4.48%	35.47
SYSCO	2.18%	$1.80	47.12%	10.89%	25.31

T. Rowe Price Group	2.24%	$3.04	35.14%	10.06%	17.23
Target	2.31%	$2.64	38.37%	2.66%	18.23
The Coca-Cola	2.73%	$1.60	71.11%	2.63%	32.58
United Technologies	1.93%	$2.94	33.79%	2.63%	23.88
VF	2.28%	$1.92	53.93%	0.00%	26.25
W W Grainger	1.83%	$5.76	32.95%	0.00%	18.43
Walgreens Boots Alliance	3.53%	$1.83	31.23%	5.69%	12.72
Walmart	1.82%	$2.12	42.48%	1.29%	23.23 [1]

Historical data of dividend yield growth per company [2]

Company Name	No. of Years	Dividend Yield	Current Price	Annual Dividend
American States Water	65	1.36%	$89.97	$1.2200
Dover Corp.	64	1.70%	$116.45	$1.9600
Northwest Natural Gas	64	2.51%	$75.58	$1.9100
Genuine Parts	63	3.17%	$96.58	$3.0500

[1] https://www.marketbeat.com/dividends/aristocrats/
[2] https://www.dividend.com/dividend-stocks/10-year-dividend-increasing-stocks/

Emerson Electric	63	2.71%	$74.43	$2.0000
Procter & Gamble	63	2.39%	$126.03	$2.9836
3M	61	3.24%	$165.58	$5.7600
Cincinnati Financial	59	2.14%	$105.35	$2.2400
Johnson & Johnson	57	2.55%	$149.50	$3.8000
Lowe's	57	1.84%	$121.15	$2.2000
Lancaster Colony Corp.	57	1.72%	$159.93	$2.8000
Coca-Cola Co.	57	2.78%	$57.01	$1.6000
Illinois Tool Works	56	2.47%	$175.86	$4.2800
Colgate-Palmolive	56	2.45%	$69.71	$1.7200
Chubb Limited	54	1.99%	$150.96	$3.0000
Hormel Foods	53	1.99%	$47.05	$0.9300
Tootsie Roll	53	1.05%	$34.12	$0.3600
ABM Industries	52	1.90%	$39.12	$0.7400
Federal Realty Investment Trust REIT	52	3.30%	$127.23	$4.2000
Stepan Co.	52	1.07%	$102.07	$1.1000
Target	52	2.29%	$115.44	$2.6400
Stanley Black & Decker, Inc.	52	1.64%	$166.35	$2.7600

California Water Services Group	52	1.49%	$53.19	$0.7900
SJW Corp	52	1.61%	$74.16	$1.2000
Commerce Bank shares	51	1.54%	$68.30	$1.0400
Black Hills Corp	50	2.59%	$82.85	$2.1400
H.B. Fuller Co.	50	1.33%	$48.56	$0.6400
National Fuel Gas Co.	49	3.93%	$42.79	$1.7400
Sysco Corp	49	2.15%	$82.67	$1.8000
Becton Dickinson	48	1.13%	$282.26	$3.1600
Leggett & Platt	48	3.22%	$50.21	$1.6000
Mine Safety Applications	48	1.23%	$138.64	$1.6800
Tennant Co.	48	1.06%	$80.72	$0.8800
Universal Corp	48	5.65%	$53.41	$3.0400
W.W.Grainger	48	1.79%	$323.45	$5.7600
Abbott Labs	47	1.61%	$89.54	$1.4400
Gorman-Rupp	47	1.54%	$37.73	$0.5800
PepsiCo	47	2.66%	$142.44	$3.8200
PPG Industries	47	1.62%	$124.03	$2.0400
V.F. Corporation	47	2.25%	$83.63	$1.9200
AbbVie Inc.	47	5.62%	$83.77	$4.7200
Middlesex Water Co.	47	1.54%	$66.30	$1.0250

Helmerich Payne	47	7.03%	$40.64	$2.8400
Kimberly-Clark	47	2.97%	$144.89	$4.2800
Nucor Corporation	46	3.11%	$49.47	$1.6100
Automatic Data Processing	45	2.07%	$178.30	$3.6400
Telephone & Data Systems	45	2.62%	$24.30	$0.6600
Consolidated Edison	45	3.28%	$94.18	$3.0600
Wal-Mart Stores	45	1.83%	$116.60	$2.1200
RPM International	45	1.94%	$72.98	$1.4400
MGE Energy	44	1.76%	$80.46	$1.4100
Walgreens Boots Alliance, Inc.	44	3.43%	$52.78	$1.8300
Pentair Inc.	43	1.62%	$44.28	$0.7600
Archer Daniels Midland Co.	43	3.27%	$42.66	$1.4000
McDonald's	43	2.34%	$210.39	$5.0000
Carlisle Co.	43	1.29%	$156.39	$2.0000
RLI Corp	43	1.00%	$94.87	$0.9200
Clorox Co.	42	2.65%	$156.07	$4.2400
Medtronic, Inc.	42	1.79%	$119.18	$2.1600
Sherwin Williams	41	0.76%	$591.05	$4.5200

Eaton Vance	39	3.28%	$46.62	$1.5000
Community Trust Bancorp	39	3.38%	$44.64	$1.5200
Sonoco Products	39	2.90%	$58.38	$1.7200
Franklin Resources	38	4.38%	$25.09	$1.0800
Old Republic International Corp	38	3.53%	$23.08	$0.8000
Weyco Group	38	3.98%	$23.93	$0.9600
Air Products & Chemicals	37	2.30%	$236.45	$5.3600
Exxon Mobil	37	5.21%	$64.74	$3.4800
Aflac	37	2.08%	$52.37	$1.0800
Atmos Energy	37	1.98%	$116.31	$2.3000
Cintas Corporation	37	0.92%	$277.96	$2.5500
Brown-Forman	35	0.99%	$70.47	$0.6972
Donaldson Company	35	1.59%	$53.18	$0.8400
AT&T	35	5.38%	$38.58	$2.0800
Ecolab Inc.	34	0.96%	$198.18	$1.8800
First Source Corporation	34	2.34%	$48.79	$1.1600
Brady Corp	34	1.54%	$56.89	$0.8700
Mercury General	34	5.24%	$48.83	$2.5200
Chevron Corp	34	4.31%	$111.12	$4.7600

UGI Corp	34	2.95%	$43.00	$1.3000
Universal Health Realty Income Trust REIT	34	2.19%	$125.95	$2.7400
Tompkins Financial	34	2.28%	$87.95	$2.0800
McCormick & Co.	33	1.44%	$166.06	$2.4800
T. Rowe Price	33	2.28%	$131.30	$3.0400
First Financial Corp	33	2.38%	$42.80	$1.0400
Cullen Frost Bankers Inc.	27	3.09%	$92.88	$2.8400
Tanger Factory Outlet REIT	27	8.66%	$14.95	$1.4200
West Pharma Services	27	0.41%	$157.33	$0.6400
John Wiley & Sons	26	2.94%	$45.97	$1.3600
Essex Property Trust REIT	26	2.52%	$308.41	$7.8000
Expeditors International	25	1.35%	$73.85	$1.0000
Erie Indemnity	24	2.31%	$167.75	$3.8600
Artesian Resources Corp. - Ordinary Shares - Class B	24	2.63%	$38.00	$0.9984

New Jersey Resources Corp.	24	2.87%	$43.15	$1.2500
Realty Income Corp REIT	24	3.61%	$78.13	$2.7900
TJX Companies	23	1.47%	$61.30	$0.9200
General Dynamics Corporation	22	2.23%	$183.63	$4.0800
Southside Bancshares	22	3.37%	$36.09	$1.2400
Computer Services, Inc.	21	1.65%	$51.30	$0.8400
First Robinson Financial Corp.	21	1.97%	$62.01	$1.2000
CCFNB Bancorp Inc.	21	3.20%	$49.15	$1.5600
Roper Industries	21	0.54%	$377.90	$2.0500
Enterprise Products Partners L.P.MLP	21	6.61%	$27.24	$1.7800
Urstadt Biddle Properties REIT	20	4.60%	$23.42	$1.1200
Muncy Bank Financial Inc	20	3.41%	$42.00	$1.4000
IBM Corp	20	4.67%	$139.55	$6.4800
Owens & Minor	20	0.15%	$6.65	$0.0100

Brown & Brown, Inc.	19	0.82%	$44.65	$0.3400
Nu Skin Enterprises	19	3.92%	$34.55	$1.4800
W.P. Carey Inc. REIT	19	4.93%	$83.77	$4.1520
Badger Meter	18	1.12%	$61.45	$0.6800
National Bank shares	18	3.47%	$41.38	$1.4400
McGrath Rent Corp	18	1.94%	$79.00	$1.5000
Republic Bancorp	18	2.62%	$44.48	$1.1440
The J.M. Smucker Company	18	3.25%	$106.27	$3.5200
Vanguard Total Stock Market ETFETF	18	2.10%	$166.17	$3.5420
York Water	18	1.45%	$48.78	$0.7208
Banc First Corp	18	2.15%	$59.53	$1.2800
Bunge Ltd.	18	3.86%	$51.61	$2.0000
Donegal Group Inc. Cl B	18	4.06%	$12.40	$0.5100
Microchip Technology	18	1.33%	$104.20	$1.4660
Farmers & Merchants Bancorp	18	1.86%	$770.54	$14.3000

Southern Company	18	3.60%	$70.05	$2.4800
Atrion Corp	17	0.86%	$717.93	$6.2000
Avista Corp.	17	3.12%	$49.99	$1.5500
Oil-Dri Corp of Americia	17	2.74%	$35.80	$1.0000
Lockheed Martin	17	2.22%	$437.17	$9.6000
Lindsay Corporation	17	1.21%	$101.95	$1.2400
Casey's General Stores	17	0.77%	$163.49	$1.2800
Harris Corp	17	0.00%	$189.13	$0.0000
ONEOK Inc.MLP	17	4.90%	$75.05	$3.7400
Occidental Petroleum	17	7.43%	$41.20	$3.1600
Calvin b. Taylor Bankshares, Inc.	17	3.47%	$35.75	$1.2400
Perrigo Company	17	1.41%	$59.52	$0.8400
Ritchie Bros. Auctioneers	17	1.85%	$43.20	$0.8000
Costco	16	0.84%	$310.85	$2.6000
Chesapeake Utilities	16	1.69%	$95.86	$1.6200
Holly Energy Partners L.P.MLP	16	11.25%	$23.69	$2.6900

Microsoft	16	1.22%	$165.46	$2.0400
Texas Instruments	16	2.68%	$128.04	$3.6000
VSE Corp	16	1.05%	$32.90	$0.3600
Waste Management	16	1.69%	$121.05	$2.0500
Assurant, Inc.	16	1.97%	$129.49	$2.5200
Albemarle Corp	16	1.86%	$80.20	$1.4700
Bank Of Utica - Ordinary Shares (Non Vtg.)	16	3.56%	$435.00	$15.5000
Eagle Financial Services, Inc.	16	3.30%	$31.50	$1.0400
Delhi Bank Corp	16	2.18%	$33.25	$0.7296
J.B. Hunt	16	0.94%	$112.86	$1.0800
Jack Henry & Associates	16	1.07%	$150.05	$1.6000
Lincoln Electric	16	2.15%	$93.13	$1.9600
Silgan Holdings	16	1.39%	$31.42	$0.4400
Prosperity Bancshares	16	2.66%	$67.72	$1.8400
Xcel Energy	16	2.42%	$67.22	$1.6200
Westlake Chemical Co.	16	1.55%	$64.20	$1.0500
Rollins Corp	16	1.15%	$36.73	$0.4200

Robert Half International	16	1.98%	$61.05	$1.2400
Torrington Water Co.	16	3.12%	$41.00	$1.2800
Edison International	15	3.35%	$76.80	$2.5500
BOK Financial	15	2.55%	$80.31	$2.0400
iShares S&P 1500 Index Fund (ETF)ETF	15	2.02%	$73.77	$1.4725
Bank Of Utica	15	2.73%	$567.27	$15.5000
Hawkins, Inc	15	2.20%	$42.35	$0.9200
Kellogg Co.	15	3.30%	$68.98	$2.2800
Landstar Systems	15	0.66%	$112.08	$0.7400
Lyons Bancorp, Inc.	15	3.26%	$38.77	$1.2400
Royal Gold Inc.	15	0.99%	$111.72	$1.1200
UMB Financial	15	1.87%	$65.35	$1.2400
Verizon	15	4.07%	$60.70	$2.4600
Alerus Financial Corp	15	2.49%	$21.49	$0.5600
AmerisourceBergen Corp	15	1.83%	$89.11	$1.6000
Cass Information Systems	15	1.90%	$56.84	$1.0800
J&J Snack Foods	15	1.25%	$165.01	$2.3000

Graco Inc.	15	1.36%	$55.05	$0.7000
General Mills	15	3.68%	$53.01	$1.9600
Cardinal Health	15	3.61%	$53.80	$1.9244
Digital Realty Trust REIT	15	3.35%	$129.82	$4.3200
Renaissance Re Holdings	15	0.71%	$189.94	$1.3600
Church & Dwight	14	1.26%	$72.02	$0.9100
American Financial Group	14	1.66%	$109.20	$1.8000
Flowers Foods	14	3.48%	$21.58	$0.7600
iShares Core S&P U.S. Growth ETFETF	14	1.49%	$69.95	$1.0260
Portland General Electric	14	2.57%	$60.91	$1.5400
Raytheon Co.	14	1.64%	$227.62	$3.7700
A.O. Smith	14	2.19%	$45.49	$0.9600
Jardine Strategic Holdings Ltd.	14	0.00%	$32.27	$0.0000
Northeast Indiana Bancorp Inc.	14	2.63%	$41.00	$1.0800
Alliant Energy	14	2.58%	$59.15	$1.5200
CenterPoint Energy	14	4.39%	$26.31	$1.1500

Technology Select Sector SPDRETF	14	1.20%	$96.93	$1.1787
First of Long Island Corp	13	3.09%	$23.13	$0.7200
First Community Financial Corp	13	4.88%	$22.11	$1.0800
C.H. Robinson Worldwide	13	2.60%	$77.88	$2.0400
Duke Energy	13	3.93%	$96.21	$3.7800
Axis Capital Holdings	13	2.65%	$62.26	$1.6400
OGE Energy	13	3.38%	$45.79	$1.5500
Tomra Systems ASA	13	0.00%	$28.80	$0.0000
Aaron's Inc.	13	0.26%	$62.77	$0.1600
Kerry Group Plc - Ordinary Shares - Class A	13	0.76%	$129.85	$0.9840
People's United Financial	13	4.42%	$15.85	$0.7100
Ross Stores	13	0.86%	$114.48	$1.0200
Broadridge Financial Solutions	12	1.67%	$129.77	$2.1600
Warrior Met Coal Inc.	12	1.02%	$19.56	$0.2000
Healthcare Services Group	12	3.05%	$26.25	$0.8000

Hillenbrand Inc.	12	2.85%	$30.23	$0.8500
Northrop Grumman	12	1.38%	$381.84	$5.2800
Aqua America Inc.	12	1.80%	$52.15	$0.9372
Experian Plc	12	1.84%	$35.36	$0.6500
The Ensign Group	12	0.45%	$45.78	$0.2000
Philip Morris International	12	5.37%	$84.68	$4.6800
Thomson Reuters	12	1.83%	$80.38	$1.4400
Evercore Partners	11	3.18%	$73.49	$2.3200
Chemed Corp	11	0.27%	$477.97	$1.2800
Coca-Cola European Partners Plc.ADR	11	2.61%	$52.99	$1.3800
Artesian Resources	11	2.56%	$39.25	$0.9984
American Water Works Company	11	1.48%	$135.80	$2.0000
Invesco Ltd.	11	7.01%	$17.97	$1.2400
Prudential Financial	11	4.19%	$92.00	$4.0000
North Western Corp.	11	3.05%	$75.87	$2.3000
Quaint Oak Bancorp Inc	11	2.40%	$15.00	$0.3600

Power Shares QQQETF	11	0.82%	$221.45	$1.8306
Travelers Co.	11	2.44%	$134.39	$3.2800
Western Gas Partners L.P.MLP	11	12.99%	$18.18	$2.4880
Arrow Financial	11	2.90%	$35.82	$1.0400
Bank of Marin Bancorp	11	2.02%	$45.50	$0.9200
Monro Muffler	11	1.18%	$70.85	$0.8800
Horace Mann Educators	11	2.67%	$43.52	$1.1500
New Market Corp	11	1.64%	$448.21	$7.6000
Altria Group	11	6.65%	$50.17	$3.3600
Isabella Bank Corp	11	4.46%	$24.25	$1.0800
Dominion Resources	11	4.51%	$84.52	$3.7600
Kroger	11	2.26%	$28.33	$0.6400
Unum Group	11	3.98%	$27.34	$1.1400
Visa	11	0.58%	$202.85	$1.2000
Ryder System	11	4.23%	$49.80	$2.2400
Techtronic Industries Co. Ltd. - ADR	11	1.26%	$41.33	$0.5340
iShares Dow Jones Select Dividend	10	3.40%	$105.63	$3.5660

Index Fund ETF				
Eaton Corp	10	3.00%	$96.27	$2.8400
BlackRock, Inc.	10	2.52%	$529.97	$13.2000
Caterpillar Inc.	10	3.04%	$136.74	$4.1200
Cummins Inc.	10	3.18%	$166.08	$5.2440
CSX Corp	10	1.28%	$76.22	$0.9600
Cognex	10	0.40%	$54.91	$0.2200
Chico's FAS	10	9.23%	$3.99	$0.3500
Armanino Foods Of Distinction Inc.	10	2.95%	$3.25	$0.1000
TD Ameritrade	10	2.60%	$48.35	$1.2400
FedEx	10	1.75%	$148.40	$2.6000
Analog Devices	10	1.92%	$114.31	$2.1600
Applied Industrial Technologies	10	1.99%	$65.56	$1.2800
Bar Harbor Bank shares	10	3.82%	$22.91	$0.8800
Hershey Company	10	2.02%	$152.19	$3.0920
HEICO Corp	10	0.13%	$123.16	$0.1600
Hasbro Inc.	10	2.62%	$104.99	$2.7200
iShares Russell Top 200 Growth Index Fund ETF	10	1.03%	$100.17	$1.0196

iShares Dow Jones U.S. Total Market Index Fund ETF	10	1.84%	$162.30	$2.9612
Oxford Industries	10	2.03%	$70.97	$1.4800
Pfizer	10	3.73%	$38.14	$1.5200
Quaker Chemical	10	0.92%	$169.00	$1.5400
Norfolk Southern	10	1.80%	$204.76	$3.7600
National Retail Properties REIT	10	3.64%	$56.49	$2.0600
Omnicom Group	10	3.30%	$76.76	$2.6000
Maxim Integrated Products	10	3.02%	$62.09	$1.9200
MDU Resources Group	10	2.76%	$29.67	$0.8300
Lakeland Bancorp	10	2.98%	$16.73	$0.5000
Marsh & McLennan Corporation	10	1.59%	$115.14	$1.8200
Republic Services	10	1.72%	$94.36	$1.6200
Retail Opportunity	10	4.48%	$17.13	$0.7880

Investments Corp REIT				
Rockwell Automation	10	2.02%	$196.67	$4.0800
Risk George Industries, Inc. - Ordinary Shares - Class A	10	3.81%	$10.50	$0.4000
Simon Property Group REIT	10	5.70%	$139.99	$8.4000
SPDR Series Trust - SPDR Portfolio Large Cap ETF	10	1.93%	$38.44	$0.7516
Standex International Corp	10	1.12%	$76.91	$0.8800
UDG Healthcare Plc	10	0.82%	$10.85	$0.0892
Union Pacific	10	2.07%	$179.64	$3.8800
UDR Inc. REIT	10	2.84%	$48.20	$1.3700
Domtar Corp	10	4.60%	$36.76	$1.8200
UnitedHealth Group	10	1.44%	$285.87	$4.3200
Tri-Continental Corp.	10	11.19%	$28.67	$3.2460
Taubman Centers REIT	10	8.55%	$28.50	$2.7000
SPDR S&P 500ETF	10	1.89%	$326.89	$6.2800

Charles Schwab U.S. Broad Market ETFETF	10	2.33%	$78.06	$1.8492
Susquehanna Community Financial Inc	10	8.27%	$19.80	$1.6400
Spirent Communicatio ns Plc - ADR	10	1.09%	$12.19	$0.1379
Six Flags Entertainment	10	8.91%	$37.73	$3.3200
Vanguard Information Tech ETFETF	10	1.00%	$258.88	$2.6052
Waste Connections	10	0.76%	$98.25	$0.7400
WR Berkley Corporation	10	0.62%	$72.37	$0.4400
Williams Sonoma	10	2.54%	$74.72	$1.9200
Ameriprise Financial	10	2.39%	$165.12	$3.8800
Compagnie financiere Richemont SA - ADR	10	1.53%	$7.57	$0.1152
Brookfield Infrastructure Partners L.P.MLP	10	3.71%	$54.49	$2.0100
Autoliv Inc.	10	3.34%	$78.24	$2.4800

Broadcom Limited	10	4.21%	$318.31	$13.0000
Coca-Cola European Partners Plc	10	0.00%	$46.72	$0.0000
Cracker Barrel	10	3.33%	$156.86	$5.2000
Bristol-Myers Squibb	10	2.83%	$64.81	$1.8000
Henderson Land Development Co. Ltd. - ADR	10	2.24%	$4.65	$0.1024
Hawthorn Bancshares	10	2.00%	$23.58	$0.4800
National Health Investors REIT	10	4.89%	$85.38	$4.2000
Moody's Corp	10	0.78%	$260.19	$2.0000
NextEra Energy, Inc.	10	1.92%	$265.81	$5.0000
Littelfuse Inc.	10	1.04%	$186.77	$1.9200
Legg Mason	10	4.16%	$39.50	$1.6000
Magellan Midstream Partners L.P.MLP	10	6.35%	$63.91	$4.1100
Industria De Diseno Textil SA	10	2.58%	$34.10	$0.8800

Kentucky Bancshares, Inc.	10	2.92%	$23.25	$0.6800
Franklin Electric	10	1.05%	$59.95	$0.6200
Idex Corp	10	1.18%	$171.28	$2.0000
International Flavors & Fragrances	10	2.24%	$135.45	$3.0000
Iron Mountain REIT	10	7.82%	$31.96	$2.4740
Group 1 Automotive	10	1.12%	$104.49	$1.1600
Pioneer Bank shares Inc	10	3.05%	$28.86	$0.8800
Omega HealthCare Investors Inc. REIT	10	6.20%	$43.40	$2.6800
KLA Tencor	10	2.00%	$175.93	$3.4000
Northrim Ban Corp	10	3.50%	$37.97	$1.3200
United Parcel Service	10	3.28%	$115.37	$3.8400
Scotts Miracle-Gro Co.	10	2.14%	$109.30	$2.3200
Steris Corp	10	0.97%	$151.05	$1.4800
Snap-On	10	2.56%	$164.80	$4.3200
Paccar Inc.	10	1.65%	$76.77	$1.2800
Health Care Select Sector SPDRETF	10	1.62%	$102.18	$1.6876

Vanguard Mid-Cap ETFETF	10	2.16%	$181.08	$3.9648
Regal-Beloit Corp	10	1.42%	$81.70	$1.2000
SEI Investments	10	1.07%	$63.45	$0.7000
Thor Industries	10	1.92%	$82.08	$1.6000
Tiffany & Co.	10	1.73%	$134.09	$2.3200

REITS

Real Estate Investment Trusts (REITs)

The REITs operate differently from other securities. Companies under the REITs umbrella are obliged to pay out 90 percent of their earnings to the shareholders in the form of dividends. Various REIT options are available in the market and the investor is required to carry out extensive research because not all companies yield higher payouts.

REITs require the shareholders to pay tax and therefore the companies are exempt from doing so. These are considered to be relatively safe investments and are often significantly influenced by market conditions and recession but otherwise the yields are lucrative. Historically, REITs have provided reliable returns on income, enabled wealth accumulation, protection from inflation as well as reduced portfolio volatility.

Top REIT Dividend Stocks [3]

Brookfield Property REIT Inc Class AREIT	6.97%	$19.14	$1.3200	2019-11-27	2019-12-31
Kite Realty Group	6.96%	$18.36	$1.2700	2019-12-19	2019-12-27
Taubman Centers, Inc. Preferred Shares Series J	6.30%	$25.68	$1.6250	2019-12-13	2019-12-31
Ramco-Gershenson Properties Trust Preferred Shares	6.12%	$58.91	$3.6250	2019-12-19	2020-01-02
SITE Centers Corp.	5.89%	$13.23	$0.8000	2019-12-12	2020-01-07
Simon Property Group	5.70%	$139.99	$8.4000	2019-11-14	2019-11-29
Kimco Realty Corp	5.56%	$20.20	$1.1200	2019-12-31	2020-01-15
Brixmor Property Group Inc	5.50%	$20.79	$1.1400	2020-01-03	2020-01-15
Weingarten Realty	5.10%	$30.48	$1.5800	2019-12-05	2019-12-13
Monmouth Real Estate Investment Corp	4.60%	$14.84	$0.6800	2020-02-14	2020-03-16
Getty Realty Corp	4.58%	$32.18	$1.4800	2019-12-24	2020-01-09

[3] https://www.dividend.com/dividend-stocks/financial/reit-retail/#tm=3-industry-stocks&r=ES%3A%3ADividendStock%3A%3AStock%23RPT-PR-D--NYSE&f_2=reit-retail

Retail Opportunity Investments Corp	4.48%	$17.13	$0.7880	2019-12-13	2019-12-30
Urban Edge Properties	4.44%	$19.41	$0.8800	2019-12-13	2019-12-31

New investors are often suggested to begin their investment portfolio with the accumulation of stocks. The safe and stable dividend income generation happens through utility organizations or the telecommunication sector. These companies are known for their high dividend yield as well as the ability to encounter economic instability. Companies such as Verizon and AT&T have a higher payout ratio of over 6% whereas Duke Energy pays 5% or above to its investors.

In order to build a stellar dividend portfolio, you need to find the top companies offering high dividend yield for its stocks. Consider companies that have high corporate earnings and share a significant amount of the earnings with the shareholders as dividends. You should invest some time and effort in understanding how various sectors perform and which industries offer the most stable returns on the investments. You need to be on the lookout of industries that withstand fluctuation economic conditions.

Websites like www.dripinvesting.com are the ultimate source to receive the names and information of the industries as per your criteria. Another way to consider the relevant companies is to look for the industries that have always been in demand for their products and services.

Utility sector is often considered the most lucrative since no matter what the economic conditions, people will continue to purchase basic utilities. Other popular sectors include telecom and real estate; again these are basic needs and need to be addressed and catered to no matter how the economy is doing. For instance, even during economic slowdown people will still buy soaps and use communication services and therefore these industries have a higher chance of sailing through tough economic conditions.

The companies that have less predictable earnings are likely to pay because the capital might be needed in a downturn. It is also difficult for those companies to plan their cash flow in advance and the economic volatility makes the environment much more skeptical. Similarly, companies with higher predictable earnings give out more to their shareholders.

Telecommunications

Telecommunications equities are the most preferred investments and can resist economic instabilities while maintaining a stable income flow. Telecommunications is an amalgamation of various complex structures including telephones, Internet and mobile phones. The heavy dependence of people on these systems makes the sector highly valuable and no matter what happens around the world, these services are essential in staying in touch and caring about day-to-day business activities.

In the past, telecommunications consisted of national operators but with the emergence of mobile technology, companies are earning their revenues through data packages and mobile plans. These companies pay out higher dividends and have more accumulated cash and are projected to yield higher earnings in the foreseeable future. Because of the growing demand for telecommunications and services, this sector has become highly monopolized by the governments but operates as an independent business entity because of the significant infrastructure involved.

The telecommunications sector consists of medium and large-scale companies such as AT&T and Verizon. These companies are big enough to withstand the exorbitant amount of expenditure involved in the expansion, operation and maintenance costs involved. Despite the challenges, the telecommunication sector has been able to adapt technological innovations and advancements and therefore continues to yield a steady dividend payout. However, the investment must be careful enough not to consider the newly established or small-scale companies because they are often unable to maintain the maintenance cost and therefore the dividend payout and growth potential is less.

Considering that AT&T and Verizon are the key players in telecommunications sector, below is a graphical representation of dividend growth for these companies from 2009 to 2017[4].

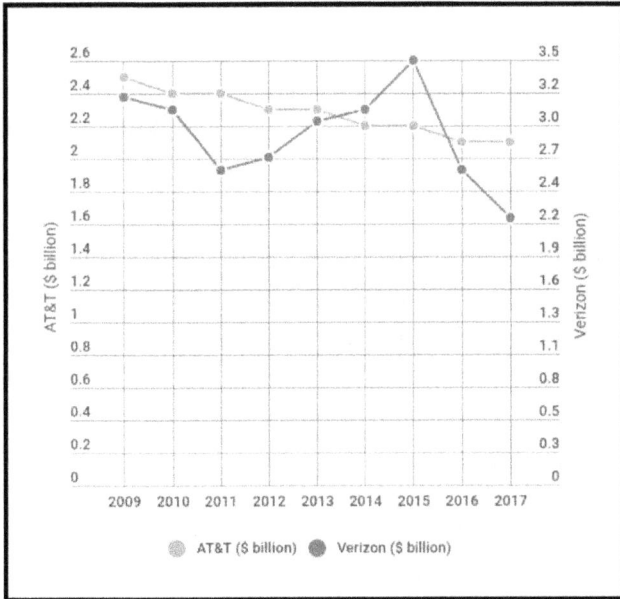

Consumer Staples

Food, beverages and items for daily use make up the consumer staples category. These are essentials that consumers cannot part ways from regardless of their financial status. Even during economic recession, these items remain in demand and therefore give out a continuous income stream. This is one of the most

[4] https://www.dividend.com/how-to-invest/7-charts-that-compare-att-and-verizon-t-vz/

favored categories for investors especially during unstable economic conditions. Well-known companies including Coca Cola, Procter & Gamble and Nestle are some of the companies that fall under this category.

Tobacco

The tobacco industry is safe, and it has survived quite a many economic upheavals in the past. Although the earnings are not even, the investors are fortunate to profit from dividend growth as well as increased stock prices. Let's consider an example to analyze this sector. British American Tobacco is reported to pay out $2.68 per share on an annual basis. The dividend yield is reported at 6.11% while the company is known to pay out 67 percent of its corporate earnings as dividends, BTI has managed to increase dividends every year[5].

Quarterly dividend history of British American Tobacco (NYSE:BTI)- 2013-2020

Announced	Period	Amount	Yield	Ex-Dividend Date	Record Date	Payable Date
3/1/2019	quarterly	$0.6745	7.11%	12/26/2019	12/27/2019	2/11/2020
3/1/2019	quarterly	$0.6745	7.11%	10/3/2019	10/4/2019	11/19/2019
3/1/2019	quarterly	$0.6745	7.11%	6/27/2019	6/28/2019	8/13/2019

---

[5] https://www.marketbeat.com/stocks/NYSE/BTI/dividend/

3/1/2019	quarterly	$0.6745	7.11%	3/21/2019	3/22/2019	5/13/2019
2/23/2018	quarterly	$0.6792	4.33%	12/27/2018	12/28/2018	2/12/2019
2/23/2018	quarterly	$0.6792	4.33%	10/4/2018	10/5/2018	11/20/2018
2/23/2018	quarterly	$0.6792	4.33%	6/28/2018	6/29/2018	8/13/2018
2/22/2018	None	$0.6740	4.33%	3/22/2018	3/23/2018	5/14/2018
12/5/2017	None	$0.5810	1.73%	12/28/2017	12/29/2017	2/13/2018
7/27/2017	None	$0.7280	2.28%	8/16/2017	8/18/2017	10/3/2017
7/27/2017	None	$0.7280		8/16/2017	8/18/2017	10/3/2017
3/2/2017	semiannual	$1.4771	4.63%	3/15/2017	3/17/2017	5/9/2017
8/1/2014	semiannual	$1.6041	2.76%	8/20/2014	8/22/2014	10/3/2014
3/3/2014	semiannual	$3.2645	6.02%	3/12/2014	3/14/2014	5/13/2014
8/2/2013	semiannual	$1.3641	2.51%	8/21/2013	8/23/2013	10/3/2013

Utilities

Utilities, like consumer staples, are another stable sector to include in a dividend portfolio. The utility sector includes companies that have a defensive business cycle that will operate no matter how difficult the market becomes. In other words, these companies will never have to close their operations even in the case of an economic slowdown. These include electricity, gas and water supplies among other basic daily utilities.

The revenue will continue to flow and since they operate on a cost-plus model, these companies are able to maximize their rate of return. For instance, water, electricity and gas will never lose their value to the people and are essential utilities in everyday use. Since this industry requires a significant amount of infrastructure, the debt is also on the higher side. The performance of their finances are positive if the interest rates are low.

Although various factors have overshadowed utilities in terms of highest paying dividends, it still remains as one of the important means of income generation for investors. The utility sector is most suitable for conservative investors, but the companies that have a higher ratio of dividend payout mean that the dividend growth potential is limited. Overall, this sector tops the list of suitable sectors to include in one's portfolio due to its unchanging and ever-increasing demand.

Master Limited Partnerships (MLPs)

MLPs encompass the limited partnership that is publicly traded. The companies that come under this sector deal in crude oil, natural gas and storage tanks. The MLPs have a higher yield compared to the utilities sector because these operate on the toll road system, in which the revenues generated are based on fee structure. MLPs consist of both energy and non-energy related companies and include gas and oil industries and also includes the industries that produce fertilizers and timber.

These companies enjoy a lot of tax exemptions; for instance, a company can qualify as an MLP if 90% of its income is generated from activities based on natural resources. Also, the revenue generated is based on the volume of gas oil that passes through the pipelines and not dependent upon the price of the fuel and therefore fluctuation in the market price of fuel does not have an adverse impact on the sector. Because of these advantages, MLPs are able to distribute high dividend payout among shareholders in most scenarios.

To Conclude

All these industries have their pros and cons. While many can withstand economic conditions, the investor is still at the mercy of a company's performance to yield desirable returns. If, for whatever reason, the company isn't able to sustain profits, the investor is left hanging dry with nothing to own as a token of its loyalty. Say a share of a dividend drops from $62 to $8 or less, there is nothing that an investor is left with. Hence, the risk factor remains high and can raise alarm at any given point.

The only way an investor can withstand these risks or ensure that he doesn't lose everything that he has invested in, he needs to invest in something more concrete, like real estate. And that is where REITs become interesting. They allow investors to skip the hassle of becoming property investors and all the troubles and processes this entails and yet be able to enjoy lucrative and sustainable profits of a real estate investor.

CHAPTER 3

STRATEGIES AND PROS AND CONS

Pros and Cons of Dividend Investing

On the one hand, where dividends are meant to benefit the shareholders, they tend to carry some disadvantages as well. You will need to know both sides of this coin inside out before you can make informed decisions. In this section, we go through all the advantages and disadvantages of investing in dividends that you, as an investor, need to understand before putting your money on the line.

Generate Passive Income

The biggest upside to dividend investing is that you can create a steady stream of income and even create immense wealth with little to no effort on your part. Sure, you will have to do your homework and be aware of market conditions to understand how your investments are doing, but in the long run, you'll just sit back, relax and enjoy the fruits of your investments, minus the labor.

Although expecting the dividend-paying companies to do good with their dividend payouts continuously may seem risky, the fact is that well-established companies and organizations tend to go to extreme lengths to keep their dividends both predictable and healthy. They go to great lengths to ensure that dividend payouts equal or exceed inflation levels year after year. Hence, they do the hard work while you enjoy the **benefits.**

Take Full Advantage of Compounding

Compounding is a pretty useful way to increase your income by investing what you earn in order to generate more earnings. It is a process in which one does not have to make additional investments to gain more earnings. Instead, allow the earnings to do the entire work for you. In the case of dividends payout, when you opt to purchase additional dividends, you are, in fact, increasing your earnings because every dividend has its own regular payout, which will continue to compound over time.

So all you really need to do is invest an initial amount and then let the profits from those investments create more profits and start the snowball rolling.

Invest Once and Profit Twice

By investing in dividend stocks, you tend to gain benefits in more than one way. We are already well aware of the regular payouts one receives while investing in dividend stocks, but they also happen to be a return on investment when the share prices increase. non-dividend-paying stocks will only benefit you once when and if you purchase them at a lower price and then sell them at a higher price. Dividend stocks, on the other hand, will provide you a share of the company's profit and allow you to retain the ownership of your investment as well. And since the well-established companies tend to be financially strong and reliable, their stock prices tend to increase over time, **increasing the confidence of their shareholders as well.**

Return Maximization with Dividend Reinvestment

We already know that you can achieve higher returns and earnings if you are using the compounding technique. However, it can be easier and more convenient if you happen to use a dividend reinvestment plan.

The dividend reinvestment plan happens to be a program that allows the investor to automatically invest their cash dividends back into purchasing additional company shares, DRIPs this way combine the benefits of both compounding and dollar-cost averaging.

These automatic purchases of shares usually occur at the payment date of the company's dividends and can be managed by the stock company itself or by a broker or an outside agent.

Full Enrollment

There may be a full enrollment in DRIP. For instance, John owns 1,000 shares of Coca Cola, and the dividend paid annually on each share is $ 1.56. The current value of the stock trade is $47 per share. The company has already paid a quarterly dividend of 39 cents.

Before John enrolled himself in the DRIP, his account would receive $ 390 on a quarterly basis. However, this time he owns $ 1,008.29 in shares. This means that the dividend of $ 390 has been fully enrolled or reinvested, whereas the fractional shares of Coca-Cola stand at $47 per share.

Partial Enrollment

John owns 500 thousand shares of a company in which the annual dividend rounds up to $3.20 per share and the trading value per share is $49. Out of the total dividend payout which John receives on a quarterly basis, he would like to reinvest and considered partial enrollment of 300,000 shares. In this case, when John receives the quarterly dividend payout, $ 160,000 will be paid in the form of cash. An additional 4,898 will also be received by John as per the following calculations:

300,000 * $0.80 = $240,000 / $49 = 4,898

Stock Market Insulation

One of the many advantages offered by investing in dividends is insulation from the stock market, which means that your investment will not, in any way, be influenced by stock market conditions. Since predicting the stock market is almost impossible and not easy, investing in dividends is a more feasible investment option for investors with good expected returns.

Dividends Mean That You Will Not Have to Sell Shares to Gain a Return

The stock market happens to be fair when it comes to valuing businesses. In other words, if the share of the company you have invested in is increasing, so will the value of your investment. But what happens when the stocks, for whatever unforeseeable reasons, take a major dip? What happens to your investment? It goes from sky-high to ground low with nothing to show for your years of investment. Say you were investing for retirement. And the dip happens right before retirement, and you are left with no money and no time to generate a stable income.

On the other hand, dividends offer regular payouts, so even in a case where the market does plunge, you will have generated a good return on your investment by then.

Dividends Support the Stock Price

It has been found that dividends support stock prices during times of recession. Dividend-paying stocks also outperform during bear markets and recessions. The reason behind dividend stocks outperforming when the market is performing poorly is because if the share prices fall, the investors will be drawn to buy more into the stocks due to the yield alone. In addition to that, since interest rates are also significantly influenced when the markets are performing poorly, dividend stocks offer risk-free rates, making them more of a viable option.

Dividends Prevent Misallocation of Capital

When investors are investing in dividend stocks of the company, they not only expect to be paid in return but also expect that the dividends will grow. Therefore, managers in such cases do all they can in order to make sure that the company is able to pay back the dividends to its shareholders and further increase their confidence.

Dividends Taxed at a Lower Rate

Dividends happen to be more tax efficient as compared to bonds and other investment options. People who lie in lower brackets do not pay federal income tax on dividends. And for individuals who are below the 35% mark on the income tax bracket, the dividends are only taxed at 15%. Even though it cannot be said that the same tax favoring situation will last forever, it definitely is a bonus for dividend investors.

Some Pitfalls and Risks Associated with Dividend Growth Investing

Twice Taxation

One of the main drawbacks of dividend investing is that the dividends are subject to being taxed twice. The first instance is when you receive the dividends because the company that is paying them is paying dividends from its net income on which it has to pay tax on annual earnings. The second instance of taxation occurs when you, as an investor, must pay personal income tax on any dividends you earn during the tax year. This means that you are paying tax twice, once being a partial owner and the other as an individual.

Growth Rate

This is an important consideration when screening companies for investments. The growth rate highlights the rate at which a specific company's stock price is affected over a period of time. Investors need to assess the history of dividend rate's growth when making purchasing decisions. Since reducing dividend rates can negatively impact the company's stock price, a company will likely increase dividends only in cases where it can sustain the higher payouts.

The growth rate is calculated by checking the percentage of the dividend that a company has increased annually.

Dividends are Not Guaranteed Unlike Interest

It is often said that dividends are the "new interest," though this is not totally correct. Interest happens to be contractually agreed, whereas dividends happen to be voluntary payments made by the corresponding companies, which can be deleted at any time. Since dividends are basically a company sharing its profit with the shareholder, a company will only pay them if it has gained any profit.

Effects of Dividend Policy Changes

When a company that is paying dividends makes certain changes to its dividend policies, especially when it comes to cutting or eliminating payouts, it is going to have a negative effect on the stock price of the company. It is a well-known fact that investors are hugely concerned with the dividend policies and any changes that may take place. Therefore, they will be drawn to sell or purchase dividends based on what changes are made to the dividend policies. If a company intends to cut its dividend payouts, the investors will receive lower earnings.

Investors Cannot Control Dividends

Unlike stocks, investors of dividends have absolutely no control over the payout methods of their investments. For instance, if the company decides to switch their payout from cash to property or liquidation, then there is very little that the investor can do to control their investment returns.

Strategies for Successful Investing

Dividend Growth Investing

Any investor is not looking at short term gains but also the long term returns for his investment. If you are investing in REITs, then you will also monitor the price of your investment. The value of stocks, as well as the value of your property, should gradually and consistently increase.

When investing in dividends, opt for companies that have a higher potential for growth. Your portfolio should include companies that are well-established and can offer consistent results, but also some companies that have major growth potential. These are relatively riskier than investing in seasoned companies, but can also offer higher returns in the long run.

A good rule of thumb would be to keep a certain percentage for investing in companies with higher growth potential. For instance, you could decide to keep 30% of your investments for such companies, and this way, if the company or number of new companies do well in the stock market, you yield higher returns. However, if they fail to grow at the desired or expected rate, then it won't break your bank.

Dividend Capture Strategy

This strategy is income-focused, where investors deal with stock trading. This is an ideal strategy for day traders. Unlike more common strategies of buying and holding consistently paying dividend stocks to yield stable income, this is a strategy that requires active trading. An investor purchases and sells shares more frequently in the hope of receiving dividends on every stock before selling them again. In some cases, this can mean holding on to a stock for just a day even.

Investors for this strategy opt for dividends that payout annually in order to generate larger payouts. This is a suitable strategy for someone who is willing to either actively get involved or would like to partner with a seasoned trader to make quick decisions regarding their investments. A trader will need to read and calculate dividend payouts on dividend calendars in order to assess the right time to buy and sell dividends profitably on a short-term basis.

CHAPTER 4

SHOULD YOU BUY REITS?

According to the reports of S&P Global Market, REIT stocks have been one of the most benefitting investments within the past decade. At the moment, the dividend yield of REITs has been 4 percent, whereas the rate per share has gone up to 32 percent. It is not wrong to say that since the Great Depression, REITs have done quite well as property investments have always been on the rise all around the world.

One such example is of Simon Property Group Inc. that has increased per share dividend cash payout by $2. Similarly, Alexandria Real Estate Equities and Omega Healthcare Investors Inc. have also reportedly increased their dividend payout significantly.

Outperformance- Reasons

In recent times, there has been a drastic decrease in bond investments as the returns remain quite low. Most investors have relocated their assets to higher dividend-paying entities and have benefited from it. Most of this relocation has been REITs due to their stable and higher returns.

Moreover, since REITs are supposed to distribute 90 percent of their income to their shareholders, the dividend payout, as well as the yields, are higher in proportion. The chart below reveals the current status of the highest yielding REITs that have continuously increased and maintained a higher dividend payout trend.

Company	Ticker	Dividend yield	FFO Yield	'Headro om'	Total return - 12 months
Macerich Co.	MAC, +2.38%	10.26%	12.86%	2.60%	-37%
Iron Mountain Inc.	IRM, + 0.76%	7.19%	6.27%	-0.92%	15%
Simon Property Group Inc.	SPG, - 0.26%	5.31%	7.97%	2.66%	-6%
Kimco Realty Corp.	KIM, + 0.68%	5.24%	6.69%	1.45%	53%
Host Hotels & Resorts Inc.	HST, + 0.06%	4.77%	10.79%	6.02%	-7%
Weyerhaeuse r Co.	WY, - 2.52%	4.67%	1.70%	-2.97%	11%
Ventas Inc.	VTR, + 0.10%	4.40%	5.43%	1.03%	39%
Vornado Realty Trust	VNO, - 0.78%	4.15%	6.61%	2.47%	-1%
SL Green Realty Corp.	SLG, + 0.15%	4.13%	8.33%	4.20%	-7%
HCP Inc.	US:HCP	3.94%	4.66%	0.72%	52%

Welltower Inc.	WELL, -0.53%	3.79%	4.48%	0.70%	52%
Realty Income Corp.	O, -0.27%	3.42%	3.96%	0.55%	44%
Crown Castle International Corp	CCI, -0.43%	3.40%	4.18%	0.78%	38%
Regency Centers Corp.	REG, -0.19%	3.36%	5.51%	2.15%	15%
Public Storage	PSA, +0.19%	3.33%	4.44%	1.11%	27%
Digital Realty Trust Inc.	DLR, +0.12%	3.20%	4.96%	1.75%	24%
Extra Space Storage Inc.	EXR, -0.99%	3.12%	4.12%	1.00%	39%
Federal Realty Investment Trust	FRT, +0.04%	2.99%	4.49%	1.50%	21%
Boston Properties Inc.	BXP, -0.13%	2.90%	5.14%	2.24%	17%
Apartment Investment and Management Co. Class A	AIV, +0.11%	2.84%	4.69%	1.85%	34%
Mid-America Apartment Communities Inc.	MAA, -0.04%	2.82%	4.55%	1.73%	45%
UDR Inc.	UDR, +0.31%	2.76%	4.08%	1.33%	33%
AvalonBay Communities Inc.	**AVB, +0.00%**	2.74%	4.13%	1.39%	32%
Equity Residential	EQR, -0.29%	2.57%	3.88%	1.31%	43%
Alexandria Real Estate Equities Inc.	ARE, +0.99%	2.55%	4.31%	1.77%	34%
Duke Realty Corp.	**DRE, +0.00%**	2.53%	4.08%	1.56%	28%

Essex Property Trust Inc.	ESS, +0.53%	2.36%	3.90 %	1.54%	40%
Prologis Inc.	PLD, -1.09%	2.33%	3.60 %	1.27%	48%
Equinix Inc.	EQIX, +2.35%	1.73%	3.85 %	2.13%	41%
American Tower Corp.	AMT, +1.01%	1.59%	3.63 %	2.04%	55%
SBA Communications Corp. Class A	SBAC, +0.01%	0.60%	3.30 %	2.69%	60%
CBRE Group Inc. Class A	CBRE, +1.59%	0.00%	3.81 %	3.81%	32%

Source: Factsheet [6]

Benefits of REITS

REITs have a lot of benefits compared to other types of dividend stocks. They are less volatile and offer a higher yield for investors. More advantages of REIT investment are discussed below.

1.Reliable Business Model

The REIT is based on a simple business model in which companies lease places and receive money in the form of rents. This amount is then distributed among the shareholders as dividends. As per the regulations set by the Generally Accepted Accounting Principles (GAAP), the REITs have to declare their earnings based on each share.

---

[6] https://www.marketwatch.com/story/these-stocks-have-the-highest-dividend-yields-in-the-hot-real-estate-sector-2019-10-24

2. No Hassles of Property Management

The investors do not have to manage the property as it is the company that does it for them. The investor just needs to invest in an equity and manage dividend payout. Being a landlord is no easy job. You have to be the handyman, the gardener and the 3a.m. problem fixer of anything and everything that can go wrong with the property. REITs offer high yielding returns but without all those hassles. On the upside, you also save money that you may have had to spend on a property manager.

3. Appreciation

The prices of real estate and property entities increase over time. Short term market fluctuations and inflation have a minimum effect upon equity stocks. And in case the real estate business does get affected, it has a history of bouncing back after a certain period of economic upheaval. In this way, the investor not only enjoys higher dividend cash payouts but also appreciation of property overtime.

4. High Distribution

REITs are required by law to distribute 90 percent of their income to the shareholders, and therefore, the dividend cash payout is more than that of other entities. The financial reports are expected to be audited, and therefore a much more transparent process is in place for the shareholders. Moreover, the investment is done on tangible assets and therefore is more secure. It has been reported that REITs have yielded higher returns compared to corporate bonds.

5. Resistance to Challenges

REITs have long survived market conditions, including economic instability and inflation, and have remained consistent in terms of rewarding their shareholders. Because the fact is, no matter how frequently market trends change, people will still need a place to live and workplaces to operate their businesses. As shelter is one of the basic needs of people, it is highly unlikely that the demand for REITs and their returns will ever be negatively affected in the long run.

6. Diversification

REITs encompass a wide range of property investment. An investor can purchase REITs in multiple different areas or types of properties, hence diversifying their portfolio and mitigating risk. This not only encourages investment in various assets but also offsets the risk of investing in one type only.

Disadvantages of Investing in REITS

REITs are a pretty stable form of investment for the most part. But just like any and all businesses, there are specific drawbacks and risks involved too. The following are some of the main risks and disadvantages associated with investing in REITs.

1. Property Tax

One of the biggest disadvantages is that the investors have to pay property tax upon the income they generate as dividend cash payouts. The percentage of property tax can be as high as 25 percent. Another major drawback is that this property tax is subject to change and continues to fluctuate. The municipality may decide to further increase property taxes in order to make up for higher costs, as a result of which, your bottom line or returns can be affected.

High Tax

The dividend cash payouts are considered as ordinary income, and therefore, are taxed as such. The percentage of tax on ordinary income can go up to 15 percent, and therefore the investor has to shell out a considerable amount of money received as dividends.

2. High Management Fee

One thing which an investor must take care of while investing in REITs is that the management fee can be considerably high. An investor must consider it as an additional expense on top of the taxes being paid. Managing properties is no easy task, and while you may not be directly involved, you will still need to take care of the operational costs that come with it.

Types of REIT Investments

Now that you have read the pros and cons of investing in REITs, you should be able to make a better decision as to whether or not they are the right option for you. The fact is, historically, REITs are on top of the best-performing asset classes out there. Investors study the FTSE NAREIT Equity REIT Index to better understand the performance of the real estate market in the United States. The average return was 9.9% during the period between 1990 and 2010. These numbers have only gone higher since then. It was recorded at 11.21% in 2013.

There are 5 types of REITs, and you will need to closely study them before making a decision on which ones of these to include in your portfolio.

Retail REITs

Almost 24% of all REIT investments are in this sector. These include freestanding retail stores as well as shopping malls. These are one of the biggest types of investments in America. There is a fair chance that most of the shopping malls that you must have visited around the country are owned by a REIT. What does that mean for you? It means you can also own a little chunk of that investment. But that's just the tip of the iceberg.

You will need in-depth knowledge of the industry, or the help of a professional retail REIT advisor to get a better understanding of how this operates. In a nutshell, the returns on this income are generated from the rent paid by tenants of the mall.

On the downside, retailers may delay payments due to poor cash flow, or if the mall fails to rent out many of its commercial offerings, then the returns will be negatively impacted. Hence, before you can blindly invest in retail, you will need to ensure that your choice of retail entity is indeed making stable profits. A little look at the entity's balance sheets and debt ratio, and you should be able to get a better understanding of how it is performing.

Residential REITs

These include properties that are built for residential purposes and can include rental apartment buildings. Again, this option, too, has its fair share of risk involved. You will need to find buildings that are located in areas where home affordability is comparatively lower. Doing so would ensure that the chances of the building being rented out all seasons would be higher.

Home affordability is generally lower in larger cities like Los Angeles and New York, as the cost of owning a property is much higher compared to smaller cities. These high costs of ownership drive people to rent out.

Property in rural areas may offer higher REIT returns in order to lure investors in, but the chances of the market fluctuating or the property remaining vacant are much higher compared to residential complexes in big cities.

Big cities are populated enough to make it easier to find tenants all year round. The declining vacancy rates and an increase in rents in recent times are proof enough that residential REITs, when invested incorrectly, can yield stable and sustainable returns.

Healthcare REITs

As the name suggests, these include the real estate of medical centers, hospitals, retirement homes, and nursing facilities. The success of investing in this type of REIT mainly depends on healthcare funding as most of the returns will be generated from Medicaid and Medicare reimbursements, occupancy fees, and private pay.

Office REITs

This is an uncommon option, but one that can yield the right returns when invested incorrectly. Office REITs generate cash flow by receiving rental income from office tenants. The main advantage of this type of structure is that once occupied; there are relatively lower chances of an office relocating elsewhere anytime soon. Of course, this isn't a hard and fast rule, but the chances are slimmer, hence leading to a more stable stream of income. Again, you will have to do in-depth research on office vacancy rates, economic conditions, and rising job markets in order to invest wisely and profitably.

Mortgage REITs

This is a lesser-known and even lesser employed option. Only 10% of all REIT investments consist of a mortgage. This is the only REIT option that profits from a mortgage rather than equity. At first glance, one might think it is a foolproof option since mortgages will need to be paid off regularly; hence there'd be lesser chances of dividend fluctuation. However, in cases of higher interest rates, the mortgage REIT book value will be lower, causing the stock prices to take a plunge too.

CHAPTER 5

BUILDING YOUR EARLY RETIREMENT PORTFOLIO

Investing in dividend stocks is no different than looking for a house to buy. As an investor, you would like to gain maximum advantage and reward out of your investment while minimizing the associated risks. In the same way, most people, especially nearing their retirement period, are on a lookout for investment plans that can fulfill their financial requirements and become a regular source of income.

Investors building retirement portfolios usually look at options like investing in bonds, real estate, dividends, etc. At the heart of all of these options is to make decisions that will be lower risk, increase profits, and be able to create a steady stream of income come retirement.

Risk tolerance is another important factor. Every investor has a different tolerance to risk. While some are risk-takers, others are more conservative or cautious in nature. Investment decisions also factor in other considerations like age, financial goals, and personal preferences.

Factors to Consider

Your Age

You can take higher risks at a younger age since you'll have time to rectify or reap from your decisions at a later stage. For instance, say you have invested in real estate when the economy isn't doing so well. But the fact is you will be gaining equity. Say you have 30 years to retirement, there is a fair chance the real estate market will go uphill at some point, and you can cash out your investment and make better decisions with your investment.

Your Goals

In order to prepare for the future, you need to know what you would like it to look like. You would be better able to plan your investments once you have planned your future. For instance, if you'd like to retire early, own your home by that time, and have a diversified investment portfolio by then, then you'd likely need to invest a larger chunk of your monthly income in doing so.

However, if you are just looking for steady cash to help maintain your simple lifestyle come late retirement, then the chances are you could get away with only investing a little each month.

Your Risk Tolerance

Some people are risk-takers, whereas others are faint-hearted. For an investor in the second category, it is important to invest in low-risk options.

Your Monthly Revenue

Investment decisions depend upon wealth as well. A person willing to invest may have bills and expenses to cover, and therefore, he must consider playing it safe. If the amount of wealth is insufficient, perhaps the best way to remain safe is to avoid making a high level of investments.

Thoughts Surrounding Retirement

In a highly volatile and unpredictable global and economic landscape, people have started to rely on secondary income options. Previously, people would not have worried much about investing at a younger age, and retirees would have plenty of options to choose from. However, the situation has changed, and people have begun to think about effective retirement investment plans way ahead of time. Some of the questions that an individual has in mind regarding retirement are:

- How much should I save now to live a comfortable life post-retirement?

- How can I make my retirement earnings last?

- How much should I save every month from arriving at a reasonable amount to cover retirement needs?

- What are the ways in which I can earn a reasonable and consistent income on my savings?

With so many questions in mind, an investor may seek answers in order to consider an efficient and effective dividend investment strategy that could yield a regular income stream. Investing in stocks is a process and consists of various steps and some important factors to be considered. The following sections will provide an in-depth analysis of the same and facilitate the retirees or near-to-retirement employees with ample information to make rational decisions.

The Right Time to Invest

The right time to invest is as early as possible, probably as soon as you finish school. Even small investments will keep earning a small but steady income and lead to compounding. Imagine if you begin saving $ 1,000 every year beginning at the age of 26 with an annual return ration of 7 percent. Within the next ten years, your savings could increase and compound many times. The earlier you invest, the higher returns you'd generate come retirement. Perhaps you may even be able to retire early!

Knowing the Right Mix

Stocks, bonds, and mutual funds are some of the options an investor can consider to have a retirement-based investment plan. Ideally, your portfolio should consist of a mix of stocks and dividends from different industries and sectors. Mutual funds and bonds are much riskier in the sense that economic volatility may impact the return significantly. However, dividend investment can help counter the risk provided the investment is made in the right companies.

Determine How Much You Want to Make?

The investor portfolio depends greatly on how much money he wants to make. This is where you determine your short- and long-term goals. Any form of investing without a plan has a very lower chances of success. So you would really need to have a plan. Know how much you want to make so that you will be able to lead the lifestyle you have imagined and planned for yourself. Say you would like to generate a cash flow of $5000 per month, then you'd need to plan and invest accordingly. The following is everything you need to know on how to make targeted calculations for dividend investments:

Calculating Dividend Yield and Ratio

The dividend yield is derived by applying a simple formula of dividing the per-share dividend payout by the current market value of the share. It is the amount that has been paid by the companies to its shareholders. The simple formula to calculate dividend yield is as follows:

Dividend Yield = Dividend per share / Market value per share

For instance, the trading value of the stocks for company XYZ is $45. This results in a quarterly payout dividend of $0.30 per share. Keeping in view these values, the dividend yield would be 2.7%. The dividend yield ratio must be calculated for the companies within the same industry. The level of dividend yield is dependent upon the type of industry as well and can be described in the following manner:

❖ Utilities 3.96%

❖ Healthcare industry 2.28 %

❖ Financial services 4.17 %

❖ Technology industry 3.1 %

❖ Materials industry 4.8%

How to Interpret the Dividend Yield Formula

The dividend yield formula is essential to provide an insight into the cash flow pertaining to the investment in the company stock. The company with a higher dividend yield does not always refer to the potential for future growth. For instance, a company that has already reached the maturity stage would have no advantage in further investing, and therefore it may payout significantly to its stockholders. There are no criteria to judge how good or bad a company is by applying the dividend yield formula, but it must be considered while taking investment decisions.

Value Trap

The company with higher yields means that the amount which it is given out to the stockholders is capital that it is not reinvesting for its growth. But this is not always the case as high dividend yield may also mean that the stock price is decreasing. This situation is known as a value trap, so the investor needs to conduct thorough research on reasons for such unusual high returns. Perhaps the falling price of stocks may reveal that the company is going through a financial crisis.

Not all companies with higher yield are bad

Some of the higher yields are pertaining to the type of industry. For example, REITs and MLPs have a significantly higher dividend yield because the state laws make it necessary for these companies to share a significant amount of their earnings with the stockholders.

But wait....

Some companies may also show higher yields to attract investors and then not deliver what they promised. Ideally, the investor must conduct an analysis of the growth rate history of the company to make better decisions.

Dividend Payout Ratio (DPR)

The term refers to the total amount that a company shares with its shareholders after receiving the corporate earnings. There are various formulas to calculate the dividend payout ratio.

DPR = amount of dividends / company's earnings

DPR = 1 – Retention ratio

Example

For instance, the company XYZ has reported its annual earnings of $100,000. The same year the company has paid out $20,000 as dividends to the shareholders. Therefore, the dividend payout ratio would be:

DPR= 20,000 / 100,000 = 20 %

According to this example, 20 % is the dividend payout ratio that the company has distributed among its shareholders, whereas the remaining 80 % is the amount that the company retains for the growth of its business and is known as retained earnings.

Net Income: $ 20,000

Retained earnings: $ 15,000

Dividend payout: $ 5,000

How to Interpret the DPR

The DPR is an important consideration for investors to determine whether a said investment is worth the time. Dividend and capital gains are two sources from which investors receive their returns.

A lower percentage of DPR refers to the fact that the company is re-investing more money into the business for further expansion. This is a suitable option for individuals looking for an increase in stock value instead of dividend payout. This is a suitable option to invest in retirement plans.

The higher level of DPR depicts exactly the opposite. It means that the company is giving out a large number of its earnings to the shareholders while retaining a lesser amount for reinvesting. Such companies attract investors that are on the lookout for dividend income rather than an increase in share price over the years.

The Sustainability Factors

The dividend payout ratio is also essential to assess the sustainability level of the dividend. It is quite rare that the companies decrease the payout ratio because that would drive the stock price down. During an economic recession, the company may be forced to reduce the DPR, especially when it has been paying more than a hundred percent to its shareholders. The company would like to retain the percentage of its earnings to mitigate the risks associated with the economic slowdown. Therefore, the company must consider the expectations of the investors and the future outcome of fluctuating stock prices while setting the DPR.

Dividend Yield vs. Dividend Payout Ratio

Both of these terms are used to measure the dividends. However, the DPR refers to the amount that the company pays as dividends to the shareholders, whereas dividend yield refers to the rate of return. The DPR is believed to be a better indicator of a company's performance as it is directly linked to the cash flow. In terms of dividend yield, it is the percentage of dividend payout by the company over a year. While the DPR is shown as a dollar amount, the dividend yield is expressed in the form of a percentage.

Strategies for Investing Based on Dividend Yields

The Relative Dividend Yields

This strategy was developed by Anthony Spare in the 1960s, the co-founder of Spare, Kaplan, Bischel & Associates, and uses the value equity strategy to focus upon the stocks that have a relatively higher dividend yield. Spare advises the investors to pay attention to these stocks although this strategy is not suitable for the investor seeking short term rewards because it is a long-term strategy stretching up on up to 5 years and is not dependent upon the assessment of past performance or future growth opportunities.

According to this strategy, investors must opt for investing in bigger companies and then let their investments mature because such companies have successfully maintained their cash flow, even during the turbulent economic situations, and therefore, are stable enough to offer optimum yields.

This strategy suggests that the stocks must be bought when their yield is 50% higher as compared to the market. Also, it pertains to less volatility because the investors hold the stocks for longer periods and considered the mature and well-established companies that have undergone all sorts of economic conditions.

The Geraldine Weiss Strategy

Known as the Grande Dame of Dividends, the leading expert of dividend investment Geraldine Weiss suggests investors buy the stocks when the yields are high and sell them at their extreme lows. The Weiss approach pertains to the blue-chip stocks and is rather a conservative strategy that uses the dividend yield asset tool to measure the value of the stocks. By doing so, an investor can know about the direction of the market as well as the value of the company.

The Dogs of the Dow

The strategy was developed by Michael O'Higgins in 1991 and referred to the concept that the dividend yield of a stock is inversely proportional to the share price. In other words, the stock dividend yield increases as the price of the share drops.

According to this strategy, the investors must consider investing in the 10 highest dividend-yielding stocks and rebalancing it every year. The strategy is that well-established companies do not fluctuate their dividend payouts according to the market fluctuations. Please note that the companies with the highest dividend yields have apparently reached the bottom of the business cycle, and therefore, the price of the stocks will increase at an exponential rate.

The Dividend Achiever List

This strategy has a simple approach as it refers to the well-established and performance-oriented companies that have a proven track record of successful business and dividend growth every year. In order to make its way into the dividend achievers index, the company must have at least 10 years of consecutive growth and must be listed on one of the well-established stock exchanges. Currently, the dividend achiever list consists of over 250 companies as compared to 19 in the Dividend King Lost and 52 in the Dividend Aristocrats list. Below is the list of Dividend Achievers for the year 2019

Holdings Ticker	Name	Sector
VZ	Verizon Communications Inc	Communication Services
T	AT&T Inc	Communication Services
CMCSA	Comcast Corp	Communication Services
TDS	Telephone & Data Systems Inc	Communication Services
MDP	Meredith Corp	Communication Services
JW/A	John Wiley & Sons Inc	Communication Services
MCD	McDonald's Corp	Consumer Discretionary
NKE	NIKE Inc	Consumer Discretionary
LOW	Lowe's Cos Inc	Consumer Discretionary
TJX	TJX Cos Inc/The	Consumer Discretionary
TGT	Target Corp	Consumer Discretionary
ROST	Ross Stores Inc	Consumer Discretionary
VFC	VF Corp	Consumer Discretionary
BBY	Best Buy Co Inc	Consumer Discretionary
GPC	Genuine Parts Co	Consumer Discretionary

TIF	Tiffany & Co	Consumer Discretionary
HAS	Hasbro Inc	Consumer Discretionary
COLM	Columbia Sportswear Co	Consumer Discretionary
PII	Polaris Industries Inc	Consumer Discretionary
LEG	Leggett & Platt Inc	Consumer Discretionary
WSM	Williams-Sonoma Inc	Consumer Discretionary
CBRL	Cracker Barrel Old Country Store Inc	Consumer Discretionary
AAN	Aaron's Inc	Consumer Discretionary
MNRO	Monro Inc	Consumer Discretionary
ISCA	International Speedway Corp	Consumer Discretionary
WMT	Walmart Inc	Consumer Staples
PG	Procter & Gamble Co/The	Consumer Staples
KO	Coca-Cola Co/The	Consumer Staples
PEP	PepsiCo Inc	Consumer Staples
PM	Philip Morris International Inc	Consumer Staples
COST	Costco Wholesale Corp	Consumer Staples
MO	Altria Group Inc	Consumer Staples
CL	Colgate-Palmolive Co	Consumer Staples
WBA	Walgreens Boots Alliance Inc	Consumer Staples
KMB	Kimberly-Clark Corp	Consumer Staples
SYY	Sysco Corp	Consumer Staples
GIS	General Mills Inc	Consumer Staples
ADM	Archer-Daniels-Midland Co	Consumer Staples
HRL	Hormel Foods Corp	Consumer Staples
K	Kellogg Co	Consumer Staples
CLX	Clorox Co/The	Consumer Staples

KR	Kroger Co/The	Consumer Staples
MKC	McCormick & Co Inc/MD	Consumer Staples
CHD	Church & Dwight Co Inc	Consumer Staples
BF/B	Brown-Forman Corp	Consumer Staples
SJM	JM Smucker Co/The	Consumer Staples
BG	Bunge Ltd	Consumer Staples
CASY	Casey's General Stores Inc	Consumer Staples
FLO	Flowers Foods Inc	Consumer Staples
LANC	Lancaster Colony Corp	Consumer Staples
JJSF	J&J Snack Foods Corp	Consumer Staples
NUS	Nu Skin Enterprises Inc	Consumer Staples
TR	Tootsie Roll Industries Inc	Consumer Staples
VGR	Vector Group Ltd	Consumer Staples
UVV	Universal Corp/VA	Consumer Staples
ANDE	Andersons Inc/The	Consumer Staples
XOM	Exxon Mobil Corp	Energy
CVX	Chevron Corp	Energy
EPD	Enterprise Products Partners LP	Energy
OXY	Occidental Petroleum Corp	Energy
ET	Energy Transfer LP	Energy
OKE	ONEOK Inc	Energy
MMP	Magellan Midstream Partners LP	Energy
HP	Helmerich & Payne Inc	Energy
HEP	Holly Energy Partners LP	Energy
CB	Chubb Ltd	Financials
SPGI	S&P Global Inc	Financials
PRU	Prudential Financial Inc	Financials

AFL	Aflac Inc	Financials
TRV	Travelers Cos Inc/The	Financials
TROW	T Rowe Price Group Inc	Financials
AMP	Ameriprise Financial Inc	Financials
BEN	Franklin Resources Inc	Financials
PFG	Principal Financial Group Inc	Financials
CINF	Cincinnati Financial Corp	Financials
WRB	WR Berkley Corp	Financials
FDS	FactSet Research Systems Inc	Financials
TMK	Torchmark Corp	Financials
AFG	American Financial Group Inc/OH	Financials
SEIC	SEI Investments Co	Financials
BRO	Brown & Brown Inc	Financials
IVZ	Invesco Ltd	Financials
ERIE	Erie Indemnity Co	Financials
UNM	Unum Group	Financials
CBSH	Commerce Bancshares Inc/MO	Financials
CFR	Cullen/Frost Bankers Inc	Financials
PBCT	People's United Financial Inc	Financials
ORI	Old Republic International Corp	Financials
RNR	Renaissance Re Holdings Ltd	Financials
AIZ	Assurant Inc	Financials
BOKF	BOK Financial Corp	Financials
PB	Prosperity Bancshares Inc	Financials
EV	Eaton Vance Corp	Financials

THG	Hanover Insurance Group Inc/The	Financials
AXS	Axis Capital Holdings Ltd	Financials
LAZ	Lazard Ltd	Financials
UBSI	United Bankshares Inc/WV	Financials
OZK	Bank OZK	Financials
EVR	Evercore Inc	Financials
UMBF	UMB Financial Corp	Financials
RLI	RLI Corp	Financials
CBU	Community Bank System Inc	Financials
MCY	Mercury General Corp	Financials
AEL	American Equity Investment Life Holding Co	Financials
BANF	BancFirst Corp	Financials
WABC	Westamerica Bancorporation	Financials
TMP	Tompkins Financial Corp	Financials
SRCE	1st Source Corp	Financials
SBSI	Southside Bancshares Inc	Financials
CTBI	Community Trust Bancorp Inc	Financials
BMRC	Bank of Marin Bancorp	Financials
FLIC	First of Long Island Corp/The	Financials
WHG	Westwood Holdings Group Inc	Financials
JNJ	Johnson & Johnson	Health Care
ABT	Abbott Laboratories	Health Care
MDT	Medtronic PLC	Health Care
SYK	Stryker Corp	Health Care

BDX	Becton Dickinson and Co	Health Care
MCK	McKesson Corp	Health Care
ABC	AmerisourceBergen Corp	Health Care
CAH	Cardinal Health Inc	Health Care
WST	West Pharmaceutical Services Inc	Health Care
PRGO	Perrigo Co PLC	Health Care
CHE	Chemed Corp	Health Care
ENSG	Ensign Group Inc/The	Health Care
ATRI	Atrion Corp	Health Care
NHC	National HealthCare Corp	Health Care
MMM	3M Co	Industrials
UNP	Union Pacific Corp	Industrials
UTX	United Technologies Corp	Industrials
LMT	Lockheed Martin Corp	Industrials
CAT	Caterpillar Inc	Industrials
CSX	CSX Corp	Industrials
RTN	Raytheon Co	Industrials
FDX	FedEx Corp	Industrials
ITW	Illinois Tool Works Inc	Industrials
GD	General Dynamics Corp	Industrials
NOC	Northrop Grumman Corp	Industrials
EMR	Emerson Electric Co	Industrials
WM	Waste Management Inc	Industrials
ROP	Roper Technologies Inc	Industrials
RSG	Republic Services Inc	Industrials
CMI	Cummins Inc	Industrials
SWK	Stanley Black & Decker Inc	Industrials
CTAS	Cintas Corp	Industrials

HRS	Harris Corp	Industrials
FAST	Fastenal Co	Industrials
GWW	WW Grainger Inc	Industrials
DOV	Dover Corp	Industrials
ROL	Rollins Inc	Industrials
EXPD	Expeditors International of Washington Inc	Industrials
CHRW	CH Robinson Worldwide Inc	Industrials
JBHT	JB Hunt Transport Services Inc	Industrials
GGG	Graco Inc	Industrials
NDSN	Nordson Corp	Industrials
RHI	Robert Half International Inc	Industrials
AOS	AO Smith Corp	Industrials
TTC	Toro Co/The	Industrials
CSL	Carlisle Cos Inc	Industrials
HUBB	Hubbell Inc	Industrials
DCI	Donaldson Co Inc	Industrials
LECO	Lincoln Electric Holdings Inc	Industrials
ITT	ITT Inc	Industrials
HEI	HEICO Corp	Industrials
MSA	MSA Safety Inc	Industrials
MSM	MSC Industrial Direct Co Inc	Industrials
RBC	Regal Beloit Corp	Industrials
R	Ryder System Inc	Industrials
HI	Hillenbrand Inc	Industrials
HCSG	Healthcare Services Group Inc	Industrials

ABM	ABM Industries Inc	Industrials
BRC	Brady Corp	Industrials
FELE	Franklin Electric Co Inc	Industrials
MGRC	McGrath RentCorp	Industrials
MATW	Matthews International Corp	Industrials
TNC	Tennant Co	Industrials
LNN	Lindsay Corp	Industrials
GRC	Gorman-Rupp Co/The	Industrials
MSFT	Microsoft Corp	Information Technology
V	Visa Inc	Information Technology
IBM	International Business Machines Corp	Information Technology
ACN	Accenture PLC	Information Technology
TXN	Texas Instruments Inc	Information Technology
ADP	Automatic Data Processing Inc	Information Technology
QCOM	QUALCOMM Inc	Information Technology
ADI	Analog Devices Inc	Information Technology
XLNX	Xilinx Inc	Information Technology
MCHP	Microchip Technology Inc	Information Technology
MXIM	Maxim Integrated Products Inc	Information Technology
BR	Broadridge Financial Solutions Inc	Information Technology
JKHY	Jack Henry & Associates Inc	Information Technology
BMI	Badger Meter Inc	Information Technology
CASS	Cass Information Systems Inc	Information Technology
ECL	Ecolab Inc	Materials
APD	Air Products & Chemicals Inc	Materials

SHW	Sherwin-Williams Co/The	Materials
PPG	PPG Industries Inc	Materials
NUE	Nucor Corp	Materials
IFF	International Flavors & Fragrances Inc	Materials
WLK	Westlake Chemical Corp	Materials
HoldingsTicker	Name	Sector
ALB	Albemarle Corp	Materials
RPM	RPM International Inc	Materials
ATR	AptarGroup Inc	Materials
SON	Sonoco Products Co	Materials
RGLD	Royal Gold Inc	Materials
SLGN	Silgan Holdings Inc	Materials
BCPC	Balchem Corp	Materials
SXT	Sensient Technologies Corp	Materials
KWR	Quaker Chemical Corp	Materials
FUL	HB Fuller Co	Materials
SCL	Stepan Co	Materials
HWKN	Hawkins Inc	Materials
DLR	Digital Realty Trust Inc	Real Estate
O	Realty Income Corp	Real Estate
ESS	Essex Property Trust Inc	Real Estate
WPC	WP Carey Inc	Real Estate
ELS	Equity LifeStyle Properties Inc	Real Estate
FRT	Federal Realty Investment Trust	Real Estate
NNN	National Retail Properties Inc	Real Estate

OHI	Omega Healthcare Investors Inc	Real Estate
NHI	National Health Investors Inc	Real Estate
SKT	Tanger Factory Outlet Centers Inc	Real Estate
UHT	Universal Health Realty Income Trust	Real Estate
UBA	Urstadt Biddle Properties Inc	Real Estate
NEE	NextEra Energy Inc	Utilities
DUK	Duke Energy Corp	Utilities
D	Dominion Energy Inc	Utilities
SO	Southern Co/The	Utilities
XEL	Xcel Energy Inc	Utilities
ED	Consolidated Edison Inc	Utilities
WEC	WEC Energy Group Inc	Utilities
PPL	PPL Corp	Utilities
ES	Eversource Energy	Utilities
EIX	Edison International	Utilities
AWK	American Water Works Co Inc	Utilities
CMS	CMS Energy Corp	Utilities
CNP	CenterPoint Energy Inc	Utilities
EVRG	Evergy Inc	Utilities
ATO	Atmos Energy Corp	Utilities
BIP	Brookfield Infrastructure Partners LP	Utilities
LNT	Alliant Energy Corp	Utilities
UGI	UGI Corp	Utilities
OGE	OGE Energy Corp	Utilities
WTR	Aqua America Inc	Utilities

NFG	National Fuel Gas Co	Utilities
MDU	MDU Resources Group Inc	Utilities
POR	Portland General Electric Co	Utilities
SWX	Southwest Gas Holdings Inc	Utilities
BKH	Black Hills Corp	Utilities
NJR	New Jersey Resources Corp	Utilities
SR	Spire Inc	Utilities
NWE	NorthWestern Corp	Utilities
APU	AmeriGas Partners LP	Utilities
SJI	South Jersey Industries Inc	Utilities
AWR	American States Water Co	Utilities
CWT	California Water Service Group	Utilities
MGEE	MGE Energy Inc	Utilities
NWN	Northwest Natural Holding Co	Utilities
SJW	SJW Group	Utilities
CPK	Chesapeake Utilities Corp	Utilities
MSEX	Middlesex Water Co	Utilities

When Do You Want to Retire?

Living off dividends depends significantly on when you want to retire as well as the lifestyle which you look forward to maintaining. For instance, an individual may have a goal to retire in his 50s and spend his time traveling around the world. This may differ for another investor that is looking forward to retiring at the standard age and wants a steady flow of income post-retirement to cover expenses. Both of these retirement plans cater to different amounts of expected income, hence a different percentage of savings and investments.

For someone wanting to retire early, they'd need to invest a higher percentage of their income on a monthly basis compared to someone looking for just a little cushion apart from their pension.

The current generation is expected to be aggressively invested in passive sources of income and have a consistent retirement plan in place. However, it is suggested that not more than 50 percent of the savings must be invested in stocks.

Four Percent Rule of Retirement

This rule sets a limit on how much a retiree should ideally withdraw from their retirement account every passing year. This rule helps maintain balance with investment and income stream for retirees. 4% withdrawal rate is considered by experts to be safe and sufficient to long term investment, and savings plans as the withdrawal will likely only consist of interest and dividends rather than the initial investment amount that can continue to grow.

Words of Caution

Although the 4 percent rule has demonstrated success in the past since the economic situation has become quite volatile, the 4 percent rule cannot be considered as an ultimate or foolproof solution. This rule also does not include taxation bills and payments, leading to higher costs.

CHAPTER 6

TAX BENEFITS FROM DIVIDEND INVESTING

What are Qualified Dividends?

When an investor buys stocks, he is liable to pay taxes on them. One can either opt for ordinary or qualified taxes. The latter is better as the percentage is lower compared to that of ordinary taxes. Qualified dividends must be issued by companies that are under US possession or listed in the major US exchange. Moreover, the investor must have owned the stocks for more than 60 days before the ex-dividend date. Dividends on entities such as bank deposits, gain distributions, tax-exempt corporations, or are held by the Employee Stock Ownership Plan and do not fall under qualified dividends.

Dividend Taxes

The difference between qualified and non-qualified dividends is significant when it comes to being taxed. The qualified dividends have much less tax imposed as

111

compared to the ordinary or non-qualified. For instance, if an investor owns stocks worth $500,000 on which he receives an annual income of $20,000 and the average yield is reported at 4 percent annually.

With respect to the qualified dividend policy, the investor will be taxed at $3,000, whereas ordinary dividend policy would make him pay around $5,600 in taxes, and therefore, significantly reducing the amount the investor will receive as an income. Below is the comparison of both types of dividends with respect to the charged tax rates.

Qualified Dividend Tax Rate	Ordinary Income Tax Rate
0 %	10%
0 %	15%
15%	25%
15%	28%
15%	33%
15%	35%
20%	39.6%

Taxes on qualified dividends have been 0 percent, 15 percent and 20 percent depending upon the income level of the investor. The only difference that has been reported in the policy is with respect to the long-term gains that are now independent of the income brackets.

As for the 2020, the eligibility criteria for taxation on qualified dividends are as below:

0 Percent Tax Bracket	15 Percent Tax Bracket	20 Percent Tax Bracket
The investor is married, maintains a joint return with spouse and has an income of USD 80,000 or below.	Income for single investors is USD 441,450	The investors eligible for 20 percent tax are the ones with 15 percent increased threshold of income.
If investor is single and income is USD 40,000 or below	Married investors with joint returns must have income of USD 496,600	
If the investor is the head of the household and income level is USD 53,600 or below.	Household heads accounting for income of USD 469,050	

Dividend Taxation Policies as Per Country

In most countries the state imposes corporate tax on the earnings of a company. In the case of the dividend payout, the amount is considered as an income for the shareholder but not an expense for the company. But it varies from country to country. Here is an overview of taxation policies of countries with the most influential stock markets.

USA and Canada

In the US and Canada, the tax rate on dividend payout is comparatively less because it is already paid by the company in the form of corporate tax.

United Kingdom

In the UK a company releases the dividend payout after paying the corporate tax which has witnessed variations from 20 % to 19% in 2017. The shareholders are expected to pay tax on the dividend income of 7.5% for basic ratepayers. The high taxpayers are charged 32.5% whereas the additional ratepayers have to shell out 38.1%. The income amount received above £2,000 is taxed and collected through personal tax returns.

India

In India, the companies have to pay corporate dividend tax on top of the income tax. In this case the investor does not have to pay tax on his dividend income provided that the amount remains lower than INR 1000, 000 over which the shareholder is liable to pay 10% of dividend tax.

Australia and New Zealand

Countries including New Zealand and Australia have the option of attaching imputation credits to the dividend and this is known as the dividend imputation system. According to the system, $1 paid by the company in tax counts as one imputed credit. This saves the shareholder from paying double taxation on the companies earning.

CHAPTER 7

BUILDING A STELLAR PORTFOLIO

You must have heard the importance of building an investment portfolio again and again. Anyone and everyone who knows anything about stock and dividend investments knows the importance of a diversified portfolio. But what does that really mean? It is a common misconception that a portfolio consists of shares in multiple different stocks rather than investing in just one company.

Sure, it is the gist of it, but a good, profitable and somewhat foolproof portfolio is one that is built on different TYPES of stocks and their payout methods among other important considerations we will be discussing in-depth in this section.

There are a lot of other factors to consider while building the portfolio such as assessing the risk ratio and looking out for the market conditions.

Why You Shouldn't Just Randomly Invest in Different Companies

Markets are extremely unpredictable. Even a controversial speech by the US President has proven to affect stock markets greatly. Regardless of how stable a company is, or how well a specific industry has been performing in recent times, the stock market remains dangerously unpredictable. From an incompetent CEO to a problem with the labor union, anything can shake up the company's stocks by large margins.

Even if you invest in a number of different companies, similar factors make random investments risky. Hence, it is strongly advised to not put all your eggs in one basket! Not to say there is a surefire or fail-proof way to build a portfolio, but as an investor with hefty amounts of money on the line, it is up to you to mitigate all risks to the minimum.

Lehman Brothers is a great example of how a successful, and apparently stable company came crashing down due to a mortgage crisis back in 2008, leaving all its shareholders hanging out to dry.

If your portfolio is diversified, you are likely to escape a few upheavals. But the secret is to make sure that diversity must reflect in the *types of industry* rather than just companies.

For instance, a drop-in *oil gas* business can still yield you with a better dividend payout from consumer staples. Considering the history of the US market, it is likely to show growth in the future as well and diversified portfolio will prevent you from bearing hefty losses. A typical diverse portfolio would look like the table below:

Dividend Stock	Sector	Yield
Disney	Consumer discretionary	1.6%
Procter & Gamble	Consumer Staples	3.7%
ExxonMobil	Energy	4%
JPMorgan Chase	Financials	2.1%
Johnson & Johnson	Healthcare	2.9%
Boeing	Industrials	2%
DowDuPont	Materials	2.3%
Simon Property Group	Real estate	4.6%
Apple	Technology	1.6%
Duke Energy	Utilities	4.5%
	Average	3%

DATA SOURCE: GOOGLE FINANCE

With thousands of companies doing well in the market, how is one supposed to select the appropriate ones? The selection of companies is an important part of building a portfolio because your earnings will highly depend upon them. It is also not possible to buy shares for every company but just selects a few based on their past performance and growth percentage. But remember, an insufficient and ineffective portfolio can increase the risk rather than avert it, so you had better be thorough with your research.

Reasons for Investing in Dividend Stock Portfolio

Of course, the primary reason for investors to invest in dividend stocks is its stability, which is more reliable compared to stock prices. During the economic recession of 2008, more than 35% of the S&P 500 stock prices lost their value, but the dividend payout was actually more during this time. An exception was witnessed during the immense recession in 2009 when the S&P 500 companies reduced the dividend payout, but even then, it was a good amount at 20%. The dividend payout again increased in the following years and reached the maximum in 2011.

Imagine an investor who had bought several stocks in 1970 would have received a significant dividend payout a few decades later. Interestingly, as inflation increased by up to 700% during those decades, the dividend payout increased by up to 2,400%.

Similarly, the inflation after 2000 increased by up to 46%, whereas the dividend payout by the S&P 500 companies has risen to more than 200%. Needless to say, the yields from having a diversified portfolio are a great weather shield for all economic seasons.

Consider the Risk Factors

When building a portfolio, make sure you consider all the risk factors involved. For instance, nobody could have predicted the oil and gas industry taking a downward turn. But a few acts of terrorism and political turmoil around the globe and the tables turned quite aggressively. To date, this specific industry remains under the crutches of political disturbance.

Hence, it is extremely important that you understand the current economic and political conditions, not just in your country but across the globe before you make purchasing decisions.

Follow investment mentors and advisors to understand better how these conditions can impact your investments.

Number of Stocks

Most investors would not believe this, but having future stocks can actually be healthy for the dividend portfolio. According to the American Association of Individual Investors (AAII), the volatility of holding single stock is 30% more as compared to a diversified portfolio.

There are certain rules to follow, which may not guarantee higher yields but will decrease the risk factors associated with such investments.

- Investment in 400 stocks can reduce the diversifiable risk by approximately 95%.

- Investment in a hundred stocks can reduce the diversifiable risk by 90%.

- Investing in 25 stocks can reduce diversifiable risk by approximately 80%.

Holding stocks lower than 50 can significantly reduce the trading cost and save the time of investors that could otherwise be spent researching various companies. Various studies conducted in this regard have reported that a safe bet would be to invest in around 25 to 100 stocks.

Financial Leverage

Financial leverage is one of the significant risk factors to consider while investing in dividend stocks. If a company has more debts, the stocks will greatly fluctuate during volatile business and/or economic conditions.

Increased interest rates are not favorable for smaller but highly levered companies because, in such situations, the credit conditions tighten as well. Therefore, it is important to consider the credit value of the company in which the investor is interested in investing because these stocks are likely going to have a high volatility level.

Considering the Industry Diversification

As highlighted before, it is highly recommended that an investor opts for a wide range of industries when building a portfolio. Ideally, you shouldn't invest more than 25% in one specific industry.

It can be quite tempting for investors to opt for a specific industry that has been yielding higher returns, or because they are interested/knowledgeable of a specific industry. But this exposes the investments to higher risks compared to investments in diversified industries.

There are certain industries, like consumer staples, that are relatively turmoil proof, but even they are exposed to various risks and thus shouldn't be entirely relied upon.

Does Size Matter?

Of course, it does. For bigger companies, there are more trading opportunities as a number of buyers and sellers are significant as compared to the companies with smaller market caps. Such companies have fewer buyers and sellers with a tighter liquidity ratio. It is difficult for smaller companies to match the price difference that bigger companies can unwaveringly offer.

It is highly suggested against investing significantly in companies with small-cap stocks because those are highly likely to outperform or underperform and have a higher volatility rate. For example, while trading stocks for Microsoft, the seller can have the advantage of having a large number of buyers that are willing to pay the sellers price.

For instance, as compared to S&P 500 and Dow Jones, Russell 2000 showed high volatility due to relatively smaller cap stocks. By investing in bigger and well-known companies, an investor can relax even during economic turbulence as such companies have a higher rate of recovery.

Standard Deviation from 1989 - 2017

Dow Jones	S&P 500	Russell 2000
14.8%	16.8%	18.5%

Understanding the Beta

The aforementioned risk factors are significant to be considered, but there is another factor as well known as the beta or price volatility, and it comes into play in the long-term holding time frame in case you are looking for significant growth in the dividend portfolio.

The price for the literacy of stocks is also significantly influenced by the four factors mentioned above. However, it must also be considered that a company that has shown a low beta trend in the past is not likely to have the same in the coming years, and that makes beta a backward-looking trend.

Know your Personal Goals

As you keep the aforementioned factors in mind, it is also essential for you to define your goals. Considered asking yourself the following questions:

- Why are you planning on investing?

- How much can you invest?

- How much risk are you willing to take and tolerate?

- Are you investing to receive regular income after your retirement?

- For how long are you willing to commit to the investment?

Once you have clarity about these factors, it will be easier for you to build your portfolio using your choice of tool.

Tools for Dividend

The advancement in technology, especially with respect to finances and the stock market, means various software and tools are in place for the new as well as experienced investors. There are many assistive tools, apps, and software available that can truly help investors make better investing decisions as well as keep track of their investments. However, not all of these assistive tools are as supportive and as helpful as one might expect them to be. Purchasing the right software or app is an important investment. The following are some important considerations when searching for the right technological support.

- It must be able to show details of all your dividend investments individually as well as an overview.

- We should be able to notify you via email or push notifications regarding any activity in relation to your dividend investments.

- Provides investor access to various dividend related published reports.

- Research and suggest investment-worthy stocks on a regular basis.

- Prevent the investor from receiving dividend cuts by providing a safe score system.

- It provides the option to export the portfolio in two spreadsheets for later analysis.

Below is a sample of what your dividend analysis tool or software display should look like.

Ticker	Shares	Price	% of Portfolio	Gain or Loss (%)	Dividend Yield	Yield on Cost	Dividend Safety	Dividend Growth	Annual Income
ABBV	225	$68.25 ▼0.1%	4.1%	67.7%	6.27%	9.26%	50	50% Very Fast	$963
ARCC	600	$18.18	2.9%	9.4%	8.80%	9.63%	59	4% Slow	$960
BUD	100	$89.34	2.4%	-18.0%	1.69%	1.38%	44	-53% Very Slow	$151
BXMT	500	$35.80 ▼0.4%	4.8%	37.3%	6.93%	9.03%	27	0% Very Slow	$1,240

Dividend Screening

To maintain a stellar dividend investment portfolio, screening of dividend stocks is an important step. There are various tools and techniques available in this regard. With the help of these tools, investors can screen equities by a selection of characteristics including annual dividend and sector rating.

The following are the most note-worthy and prominent dividend screeners.

The DARS Rating

The dividend advantage rating system is a tool that evaluates up to 2,000 stocks. The Dividend Advantage Rating System analyzes the dividends based on five metrics. Any rating above 3.0 thresholds can reduce the time and effort to select dividends options with better pay outs. A typical DARS would appear as below:

Rank Change	Stock Symbol	Company Name	DAR S™ Rating	Dividend Yield	Current Price	Ex-Div Date	ETF Alternative
1	99	ABC	3.5	20%	5.39%	$37.12	2020-01-09
3	97	XYZ	3.2	13%	6.70%	$47.11	2019-12-24
4	96	LDM	3.0	11%	2.52%	$149.58	2020-02-24

Market Cap and Sector

These are the two crucial factors to consider for picking up a successful investment plan. For instance, a company having diversified business line and increased market cap means that it can sustain its standing during tough situations. The company has the ability to increase its cash flows at any stage of its business cycle. Investing in such companies provides a higher margin for the investors with respect to future payouts.

As an investor, you must conduct a thorough research and consider companies that have at least 10 to 25 years of dividend increasing record. Certain companies including Target, Coca-Cola and Chevron Corp. have been increasing their dividend payouts regularly since the past six decades.

Strong Growth and Earnings

Another factor is to consider the companies with strong earnings and to compare that information with its technical indicators. Certain tools enable investors to rank the highest performing companies in terms of dividend payouts and provide them with the most watched stocks list. However, this feature is mostly available for premium users and provides a weekly update if certain preferred stocks are fluctuating. It also offers a live email option so investors can make faster decisions.

Dividend Stocks with Significant Track Records

Company	Sector	Consecutive annual dividend increase	Dividend yield
3M	Consumer industrials	60	2.7 %
Abbott Laboratories (ABT)	Healthcare	46	1.8 percent
AbbVie	Healthcare	46	5.4 percent
Aflac	Financial services	36	2.2 percent
Air Products & Chemicals	Basic materials	36	2.8 percent
A.O. Smith Corp.	Industrials	26	1.8 percent
Archer-Daniels Midland	Consumer defensive	43	3.2 percent
AT&T	Communications services	34	6.9 percent
Automatic Data Processing	Technology	44	2.2 percent
Becton Dickinson	Healthcare	47	1.3 percent
Brown-Forman Corp. (BF.B)	Consumer defensive	34	1.3 percent
Chevron Corp.	Energy	33	3.8 percent
Chubb	Financial services	26	2.2 percent
Cincinnati Financial Corp. (CINF)	Financial services	58	2.5 percent
Cintas Corp. (CTAS)	Industrials	36	1.1 percent
The Clorox Co.	Consumer defensive	41	2.5 percent

The Coca-Cola Co.	Consumer defensive	56	3.2 percent
Colgate-Palmolive Co.	Consumer defensive	55	2.6 percent
Consolidated Edison (ED)	Utilities	44	3.8 percent
Dover Corp. (DOV)	Industrials	63	2.2 percent
Ecolab	Basic materials	33	1.2 percent
Emerson Electric Co.	Industrials	62	3 percent
Exxon Mobil Corp.	Energy	36	4.4 percent
Federal Realty Investment Trust (FRT)	Real Estate	51	3 percent
Franklin Resources (BEN)	Financial services	37	3.4 percent
General Dynamics Corp. (GD)	Industrials	28	2.1 percent
Genuine Parts Co. (GPC)	Consumer cyclical	62	2.8 percent
Hormel Foods Corp. (HRL)	Consumer defensive	52	2 percent
Illinois Tool Works	Industrials	55	3 percent
Johnson and Johnson	Healthcare	56	2.7 percent
Kimberly-Clark Corp.	Consumer defensive	46	3.5 percent
Leggett & Platt	Consumer cyclical	47	3.5 percent
Lowe's Companies	Consumer cyclical	56	2 percent
McCormick & Co.	Consumer defensive	32	1.8 percent
McDonald's Corp.	Consumer cyclical	42	2.7 percent
Medtronic	Healthcare	41	2.3 percent
Nucor Corp.	Basic materials	45	2.7 percent
Pentair	Industrials	42	1.7 percent
Pentair United Financial	Financial services	25	4.1 percent
PepsiCo	Consumer defensive	46	3.3 percent
PPG Industries	Basic materials	46	1.8 percent

Procter & Gamble Co.	Consumer defensive	62	3 percent
Roper Technologies	Industrials	26	0.6 percent
S&P Global	Financial services	46	1 percent
Sherwin-Williams Co.	Basic materials	40	0.8 percent
Stanley Black & Decker	Industrials	51	2.1 percent
Sysco Corp.	Consumer defensive	48	2.4 percent
T. Rowe Price Group	Financial services	32	3 percent
Target Corp.	Consumer defensive	51	3.6 percent
United Technologies	Industrials	25	2.4 percent
V.F. Corp.	Consumer cyclical	46	2.4 percent
Walgreens Boots Alliance	Consumer defensive	43	2.5 percent
Walmart	Consumer defensive	44	2.2 percent
W.W. Grainger	Industrials	47	1.8 percent

Source U.S. News & World Report [7]

Sample Dividend Screener

A typical dividend screening tool would appear as below. If you notice, there are various factors to choose from while searching for preferred stocks and companies. As an investor, you may search by bargain stocks or tech giants. You may also seek information by the options of 52-week lows and highs. On the left-hand side, various filters are provided which allow investors to further compress the list by selecting choice of price, location

[7] https://money.usnews.com/investing/stock-market-news/slideshows/dividend-stocks-aristocrats?slide=55

and sector. Such screeners are eminent in maintaining a stellar portfolio as it saves a lot of time and effort from consulting a manual and independent research online. Moreover, these screeners are updated on a regular basis as they are internet integrated.

Popular Screens:	High dividend yields	Bargain stocks	Blue chips	52-week highs	52-week lows	Price shockers	Tech giants

FILTERS	+	X	NAME	DIVIDEND YIELD ▼	MARKET CAP	SECTOR
DIVIDEND YIELD (%)		⌄	EOCFF Enel Generación Chile SA	42.48	8.42B	Utilities
MARKET CAP (COB)		⌄	RELFF Reliance Infrastructure Limited	34.90	5.75B	Utilities
SECTOR		⌄	NTXFY Naturgy SA	20.70	12.21B	Financials
P/E (TTM)		⌄	EVRZF EVRAZ PLC	20.41	5.33B	Basic Materials
PRICE (CUR)		⌄				
ANALYST RATING		⌄	EXXAY Assore Resources Limited	18.79	41.91B	Energy
EXCHANGE		⌄	YZCAY Yanzhou Coal Mining Company Limited	18.03	5.73B	Energy
COUNTRY/REGION		⌄	MTLPR Mechel Public Joint Stock Company	17.36	57.80B	Basic Materials
			GRLS			

Source: MSN Money [8]

Selecting the Best Screener

Various screening tools are available with respect to the location of the investor or for the regions an investor is interested in. Stock Rover is the most favored screener for investors residing in America or Canada. For the investors residing out of these countries have the choice of using Metastock or Tradingview.

Metastock can be handy in terms of receiving technical analysis and also shows real-time news to the users. Tradingview encompasses almost all the stocks available

---

[8] https://www.msn.com/en-us/money/stockscreener/hdys

around the world and is the best choice for international investors.

Selecting the Dividend Investment Strategy

Before you decide to invest in certain stocks, make sure that you have a consistent and relevant strategy at hand. Primarily there are four main options to select from.

You may adopt the **safe dividend strategy** if you want to minimize the risk associated with stock investment. Make sure that the company is listed on well-regulated stock exchanges such as NASDAQ or NYSE. Also, consider the sales growth of the stocks higher than the dividend growth because it will be comparatively a more stable investment in the long run. It is important to make sure that the company has been paying a dividend for a long period of time and are highly capitalized.

A **high dividend yield strategy** stock is what a new investor will be looking at. But do note that a higher yield may also result in a significant drop in the price of the stock as well. While considering such companies, always make sure that the payout ratio does not exceed 60.

An aristocrat index or list of companies is important if you are investing in the **long-term** dividend growth strategy. Consider a screener that has a huge volume of historical data so that, as an investor, you have a pretty fair idea about the companies and their performance over the years.

You may also look into the ***dividend strategy + value*** criteria for screening. This strategy has been successfully used by well-known investors such as Ben Graham and Warren Buffet. The companies to look for under these criteria are the ones having low price to book, sales and earnings. Stock Rover can be of great help in this regard and can filter companies as per the lowest PE ratio within the same sector as well.

Invest in the Stocks

Once you are clear on the strategy you wish to adopt and screener to be used, the next step is to conduct research and begin buying the stocks. The user interface of this step may resemble as below:

In this step, you can also develop and maintain a watchlist according to your needs and requirements. The screener will inform you once there is any change in the stocks you are interested in. Also, this step will enable you to view the value score, dividend yield, fair value, and other relevant details.

Conduct a Thorough Research

Once you have the preferred companies on your list, make sure to check financial performance and historical growth patterns for the companies before you make a decision to buy stocks. Some screeners provide reports as well by conducting an intelligent financial analysis. This is known as the stock-rating system. It provides analysis based on:

- Dividend analysis

- Efficiency

- Growth

- Financial strength

- Growth

- Stock price momentum

Buy the Stocks

By the time you have come so far, it is safe to assume that as an investor, you have conducted complete research and are ready to invest. If your broker is charging you significantly, prefer using a non-commission-based broker. You certainly do not want to shell out a sum of money when it is comparatively easier to perform the task yourself.

Features Provided by the Screeners

The different screeners provide a lot of features so that even new investors have the ease of operating the process on their own. Some features are free of cost, whereas the advanced ones are offered only to premium members. Below are some of the features the investors are commonly provided to create their own dividend investment portfolio.

Dividend Calendar

Use this calendar to plan your annual income. This will show you the dividend payout dates as well as when to own the stocks in order to receive its dividend payout.

Dividend Aristocrats

This feature will enable you to view the most well-established stocks to own. This list is developed with certain criteria in place, and the featured companies are the ones that have shown continuous progress and improvement regardless of the economic slowdown.

High Yield Stocks

This feature is particularly suitable for investors seeking the dividend payout investment strategy. The investors can find the details of international companies offering high yield stocks.

Best Stocks

This area focuses upon the companies that have successfully grown their profits and dividend payout over a period of years.

Boost your Dividends

This feature is available for the premium investors and notifies the investor as the level of dividend yield fluctuates.

Profit Growth

The investor can find more information about the company; he is interested in investing in and analyzing the growth and performance based on the cash flows and corporate earnings.

Dividend Alarm Notification

This feature is quite helpful for investors in signaling the opportunities to buy and sell stocks on the basis of dividend yield. The investor can receive notifications in a number of choices and can stay updated without logging on the system every day.

Stock Screener

This area provides a lot of filter options for investors to choose from. All the stock details, dividend payout ratios, and yield are organized in a clear and concise format.

Rankings

The investor can creatively create rankings upon the selected criteria of their choice. The selected stocks will then be analyzed according to the metrics and produce a list of relevant stocks by creating a list through a ranking process

Important Note!

Owning dividends can be a lucrative income stream in the long run. However, there are certain other rules to follow.

❖ While buying the stocks, do not just consider the dividend payout ratio but analyze the performance of the company in the long run.

❖ The fund fees are often ignored initially while the investor is busy checking out for the most rewarding stocks to invest in. This may turn out to be an expense ratio, and therefore the fee charged must be taken into account. For instance, if stocks with the dividend yield of 4%

with the fund fees charged at 2.5 % per year, the investor is not left with many rewards.

CHAPTER 8

SAFE PORTFOLIO WITHDRAWAL

A common mistake that an investor makes, especially while the market is booming, is that they keep spending lavishly without realizing that their assets are depleting. To meet the expenses, the investors often draw money from their portfolio while it keeps on growing. Although this seems to be a positive situation, it can have serious repercussions once the market witnesses an economic slowdown.

There are various rules and strategies to adapt to ensure a safe withdrawal. Surprisingly, various studies conducted have revealed that more than 70% of American investors are not familiar with the available options.

Most of the investors have the desire to use the dividend payout to lead a comfortable life after retirement as well as to leave a considerable amount of wealth for the next generation. Both purposes are attainable provided that the investor has sufficient know-how of the outcomes of withdrawal on the overall dividend portfolio. The

139

following section will cover the important steps for annual dividend withdrawal.

First of all, the investor must consider developing an annual expense sheet with all the possible expenses he or she will incur within the year. Once this is done, any income derived from other resources such as social security or pension must be recorded as well, and the expenses must be subtracted. The remaining amount will be the expenses that the investor will be taking out of the portfolio. This amount will be known as the withdrawal rate and will be deducted as part of the portfolio value. The time horizon is an important factor to consider, which refers to the life expectancy of the investor or the dependents.

The 4% Rule

In 1994, William Bengen proposed the four percent safe withdrawal rule according to which it is assumed that the stock investments will be on the safer side if the annual withdrawal rate of 4% is maintained. This means that the investor will not be outliving his portfolio.

Reasons for Dividend Withdrawal

In order to keep the dividend portfolio safe, the investor should consider not increasing the withdrawal rate every year. When the market has a recession or goes through an economic slowdown, it is important to reduce the withdrawal rate to mitigate any financial losses. The rate can then be picked up once the market maintains its normal levels. If your life expectancy is less than 15%, it is advisable to keep the withdrawal rate lower than 4%.

Selling a Dividend Stock

There may be various situations where the investor would like to sell the dividend stocks. However, it is advisable not to do so, especially in the case of high dividend-yielding companies with a consistent track record of growth.

However, there may be specific scenarios or needs of an investor that may require him to sell dividend stock. The following are a few insider tips to help you sell your dividend stock at the right time.

There are many reasons to sell the dividend stocks, including the following:

1- There may be times when a company may decide to reduce or eliminate the dividend payout. For instance, during the economic recession of 2008 and 2009, most of the companies could not retain favorable earnings and therefore had to cut down on the dividend payouts. The investor must keep an eye on the regularly published stock reports that show the cash flow of the companies as well as future projections. It is obvious that the risks must be mitigated in the initial stages, and therefore it is expected that the investor conduct authority searches and consider companies that have rarely reduced or eliminated dividend payouts in the past.

2- At times, when the stocks are overvalued, it is suggested to sell them and protect the savings. But here the investor is suggested to keep an eye on the industrial sector rather than just the company they have invested in because in case the former is overvalued, all the companies under the umbrella will be affected in terms of stock valuation. Also, it has been witnessed that high stock valuation is followed by a low dividend payout period. The investor must be cautious about this in order to keep the market in his favor at all times.

3- Investors must keep an eye on the weight of the stock position. There may be times when a few of the stocks may become a burden on your portfolio.

4- During the time when the stocks of a particular company begin to show high volatility levels, it is better to sell those stocks.

5- If the investor feels that he has lost confidence in a certain company, it is better to sell the stock. Even well-established companies show a disappointing trend depending upon the direction they are headed in. For instance, .an investors may enthusiastically invest in buying stocks of Microsoft or Target. However, in the future, the investor deems that one of the companies is headed in the wrong direction and therefore presents a risk for the dividend payout in the future. This is an indication for the investor to sell the stock.

6- Last but not least, an investor may have personal reasons to sell the stocks. Some unpredictable situations may add up to the decision or in case the investor decides to invest the money in another scheme for personal needs. Whatever the reason may be, the pros and cons must be weighed up with the utmost care in order to minimize the risk of financial loss to the investor.

CHAPTER 9

UNDERSTANDING THE DIVIDEND CALENDAR

The dividend calendar is the tool or option that informs or reminds the investor about the dividend payout dates. This can be a useful feature for investors so they can have an idea about their income schedule. Although companies pay out dividends on a quarterly basis, there are a few that consider twice a year. Below is a sample table to understand the concept of dividend payout dates.

AFH Financial	Jan 30, 2020	8	Feb 14, 2020	2.08%
Ag Growth Int (AFN)	Jan 30, 2020	2.4	Feb 14, 2020	5.06%
Ag Growth Int (AGGZF)	Jan 30, 2020	1.812	Feb 14, 2020	5.04%
AGNC Invest (AGNC)	Jan 30, 2020	0.48	Feb 11, 2020	10.43%
Alaris Royalty (AD)	Jan 30, 2020	1.65	Feb 18, 2020	7.36%
Alliant Energy (LNT)	Jan 30, 2020	0.38	Feb 18, 2020	2.57%
Allied Properties (AP_u)	Jan 30, 2020	1.65	Feb 18, 2020	2.98%
Ally Financial Inc (ALLY)	Jan 30, 2020	0.19	Feb 14, 2020	2.39%

DIVIDEND GROWTH INVESTING

American Core Sectors Dividend (ACZ)	Jan 30, 2020	0.55	Feb 14, 2020	4.08%
AFH Financial	Jan 30, 2020	8	Feb 14, 2020	2.08%
Ag Growth Int (AFN)	Jan 30, 2020	2.4	Feb 14, 2020	5.06%
American Hotel Income Properties LP (HOT_u)	Jan 30, 2020	0.8451	Feb 14, 2020	11.72%
Ames (ATLO)	Jan 30, 2020	0.24	Feb 14, 2020	3.53%
Antero Midstream (AM)	Jan 30, 2020	0.3075	Feb 12, 2020	20.30%
AO Smith (AOS)	Jan 30, 2020	0.24	Feb 18, 2020	2.11%
APQ Global (APQ)	Jan 30, 2020	6	Mar 02, 2020	8.76%
ARC Document Solutions (ARC)	Jan 30, 2020	0.01	Feb 28, 2020	3.08%
ARC Resources (ARX)	Jan 30, 2020	0.6	Feb 14, 2020	8.40%
Artis REIT (AX_u)	Jan 30, 2020	0.54	Feb 14, 2020	4.48%
Atrium Mortgage Investment Corp (AI)	Jan 30, 2020	0.9	Feb 12, 2020	6.14%
Australian REIT (HRR_u)	Jan 30, 2020	0.66	Feb 07, 2020	5.12%
Automotive Finco (AFCC)	Jan 30, 2020	0.2052	Feb 28, 2020	12.00%
Automotive Properties RE (APR_u)	Jan 30, 2020	0.804	Feb 14, 2020	6.40%
Badger Daylighting (BAD)	Jan 30, 2020	0.57	Feb 14, 2020	1.63%

CHAPTER 10

SIX COMMANDMENTS OF DIVIDEND INVESTING

Even though dividend investment is a potentially great source of generating income, it isn't a surefire way of earning profits. It comes bearing a lot of risks that an investor cannot always foresee. However, there are some cautious steps an investor can take to minimize losses. These steps are the ten rules, also called the "Ten Commandments of Dividend Investing." Any dividend investor that lives by these rules can hardly go wrong with his investments.

Most investors turn to dividend investment to earn a high yield. Many fraudulent companies, in current times, are more focused on personal gain rather than investor's interests. One can expect for promising dividend returns that hardly ever payout. It is also common for them to experience some turbulence where dividend payouts are concerned. Not only this, but the investors will slowly see a decline in the value of these stocks. This is why the first commandment is to avoid seeking higher yields. A smart investor will be prepared with relevant questions when higher yields are promised. The investor will inquire about and evaluate any risks that these yields might be exposed to.

For instance, a historical analysis revealed that REITs have been stable in terms of dividend payouts. They are a lucrative dividend investment entity and seem to be the first choice for most investors. However, the payout that they make from their earnings, as per the law, is so significant (90 percent), that the REITs are resulting in inconsistent payouts. This is because the REITs are accumulating debt due to the high percentage of payout. In addition to this, a higher yield may also lead to a decrease in the value of the stocks. This means that the investor might face a potential loss in the long run.

Thou Shalt Always Reinvest in Dividends

As much as one can stress the power of reinvesting dividends, it is hard to articulate just by using words. By reinvesting your dividends and using the compounding technique, you can exponentially grow your investments. Investors can also make use of the dividend reinvestment programs that often automatically allow you to reinvest the dividends without paying a commission. With time and as payouts increase, the payouts of the dividends continue to increase as well, leading to a compounding effect that will snowball over time. However, it should be mentioned that the dividend reinvestment option does not apply to those who are dependent on dividend income, such as retirees.

Honor Thy Tax Implications

Over the years, the process and tax structure of taxing dividends have seen major overhauls, additions, and modifications of policies and regulations so that a complete and equitable tax structure could be developed and implemented. Taxes on capital gains will more often or not fall below the taxes on standard income. If you happen to follow Warren Buffet, you are likely aware of his statement that he is taxed less than his secretary. Most of his income comes from dividends, which puts those gains in a lower tax bracket compared to salary or other types of compensation, and therefore, he is taxed at a lower rate.

Honor Thy Payout Ratio

When it comes to dividends and investing in them, the payout ratio stands as the most important factor as it highlights the company's ability to return the profits or pay the shareholders the returns they have been expecting. If the ratio comes out to be more than 100%, it means that a firm is paying more than it is earning, which is basically a red flag in the long run. Even though there is no such thing as a "sweet spot" when it comes to paying the dividends, anything nearing the 100% mark is always going to be a cause for concern.

You can take Verizon Wireless, for example. Its most fiscal year showed that it had earnings of $2.24, while it was expected that the forward year was to fall to $2.79. This is another example of estimating dividends, which leads to falsely high figures. This technique uses forward year EPS along with the current payout, a number of resources will use earnings of the most recent year and combine them with the dividend payout of the current year.

The investment opportunities in the U.S market are considered to be some of the highest. It is estimated that the US market constitutes 50 percent of the global investment. Even though the US market is strong and has many opportunities, an investor should not limit himself to this market alone. An investor should consider having multiple dividend investments, foreign as well as within the US market. What this strategy does is lower the risks of loss; if one market collapses, there is always a backup dividend income in place from other regions. For instance, the growing US and China trade war may result in fluctuation. While these two countries may take a hit, it could result in increased benefits for other foreign markets. As an investor who invests in local and foreign dividend investments, he won't suffer as big a loss as someone who solely invests in the US dividend investments.

If you decide on investing in foreign dividend investments, make sure you familiarize yourself with

DIVIDEND GROWTH INVESTING

their local taxation policies to avoid any complications. In the US, tax policies are quite clear, and most investors are aware of them. One of the drawbacks of investing in foreign markets is that you won't find much information on it from people around you. Therefore, it is recommended to research as much as you can on their policies. For example, companies in the US are required by law to reveal their financial information to investors. However, this may or may not be the case for companies operating in other countries. Similarly, dividend payout policies may also differ. This is why it is strongly recommended that all investors find out all the information before taking the leap.

Once you've made sure you have all the information needed to invest in a foreign dividend investment, you might find it to be beneficial in many ways. For one, the cash payout is received by the investor in varying foreign currencies. This can be an advantage, especially if it is received from a country that has a stable and increasing currency value.

How many times have you fallen victim to the shelf that is marked with a 75% discount? It isn't easy to ignore your favorite - but expensive - truffle chocolates with more than half off. However, you bring the truffles home only to realize that they're so close to expiration, they'll go bad before you can even finish the pack. In reality, this purchase was, in fact, a loss, rather than a saving. Similarly, a company may show you high yielding investment opportunities, but not all that glitters is gold. The company might be tricking you into buying stocks with the promise of high yields when, in reality, it might be facing a considerable amount of loss.

To make sure you don't have to take a company's word for it, spend a considerable amount of time researching different companies and markets. A little time spent researching might help you avoid potentially high losses. And because large chunks of an investor's savings are invested in these companies, proper steps should be taken to avoid any hidden risks involved in dividend investments.

When an investor considers buying stocks, he should do deep research into the company's performance and dividend payouts. This is where many investors stumble. They run a background check on the company's performance in recent years. However, it makes more sense to check the record of the company for at least the past decade. A company that has a consistent increase in dividend payouts is considered to be stable for investment. Moreover, the investor must also conduct thorough research to ensure that the company has complete transparency and isn't tricking investors by showing good financial performance. The growth of dividend payouts is only good in the case that the company does not have a high debt ratio, and is consistently growing in terms of its operations and product demand.

On the other hand, companies who are constantly raising their dividend payouts are under pressure as well. This can lead the management toward making riskier investments, and therefore, it is important for the investors to pay close attention and stay put with the financials of the company.

Thou Shalt be Wary of Value Traps

Value trap, a phenomenon where a dividend may yield strong returns, and the stock might look cheap because the price might have been dropping, make the stock look like a false buy. The first sign of a value trap is a company paying excessive dividend payouts when the cash flow has been falling as compared to its competitors. Value traps happen to draw in the savviest of investors. Therefore, it is important for them to be careful while investing in stocks.

Though Shalt be Mindful of Special Dividends

A company may sometimes initiate special dividends such as a special one-time dividend payout. Microsoft, for example, issued a large dividend back in 2004. Investors should keep an eye out for such stocks as things may seem rosier than normal. There is, of course, a huge difference between a one-time payout and standard dividend payouts. One thing investors should do in such cases is to look at statistics, particularly the history of payouts. While picking out the dividend stocks to invest in, investors should look into history to observe the payout patterns and behaviors of each company.

Though Shalt Not Make Dividends Thy Only Priority

As it has been assessed that dividends are a great way to invest in a consistent stream of income. However, it should not be the only metric to abide by. Every security has a certain set of fundamentals that make it right or wrong, and many times it will not have to do anything with the payout of the dividends. Therefore, it is imperative for investors to ensure and understand how a company operates and its future position. A strong company is better than a weak company that has strong yields.

Dividend's Worst Year

The economic recession of 2008 was significantly high after the Great Depression and the stock market lost more than half of its value. The financial shock made most of the well-established companies make decisions differently from the standard and traditional rules as they succumbed to financial losses. The real estate investors and the companies faced a serious cash crunch, and because of this, the dividend payout by the companies was significantly decreased. Standard and Poor reported that more than 800 stocks out of 7,000 had to cut the payouts. Companies including General Electric, Dow Chemical, and Pfizer were hard hit over a period of many decades, and it is estimated that the investors faced the financial loss of over $58 billion.

The S&P 500 report reveals that out of the dividend-paying companies, 78 drastically cut their dividend payout to approximately 21%. However, on the other hand, a few companies did increase the dividend payouts. The 363 stocks that performed well made up 73% of the index and provided a pool of opportunities for investors. This also refers to the fact that the companies listed in the S&P 500 indexes are mostly profit-making. However, the stability issue is still not guaranteed.

Situations like these have a lot of lessons to teach dividend investors. It is important to understand that investing in stocks can be a risky business, especially if the cautionary measures are ignored.

A few well-known strategies for picking up stocks can be beneficial. These approaches can be merged in order to get better yields. There are no hard and fast rules that can guarantee a persistent income generation, but by implementing a few strategies, risks associated with dividend investment growth can be mitigated.

CHAPTER 11

CASE STUDIES- BUILDING A SUCCESSFUL PORTFOLIO

Building a successful portfolio requires patience, research, and observation of how companies behave. It is not only about buying dividends and then waiting for the yields. Instead, it is also about diversifying your portfolio so you can create additional income streams. Take Bill Gates and Warren Buffet, for example. They are still the kings of investment, and with time, have developed a habit of investing in stocks that carry the least amount of risk. Let us discuss them a bit.

Bill Gates

Berkshire Hathaway, Inc.

Berkshire Hathaway happens to be the largest holding firm in Bill Gate's dividend foundation portfolio. The foundation owns 54 million shares of Berkshire

Hathaway with a value of just under $10 Billion. Berkshire Hathaway is one of the biggest companies in the S&P 500, with a market capitalization of $51184 billion and in 2017 was ranked second on fortune 500.

Microsoft

The second-largest holding company in the foundation is Bill Gate's own, Microsoft. The foundation owns 32 million shares of the company at a value of nearly $3.12 billion. Microsoft is one of the biggest companies in the S&P 500, with a market capitalization of $825 billion and was ranked 28th on Fortune 500 in 2017.

Caterpillar

Caterpillar is the third-largest company in the foundation's portfolio. The foundation happens to own over 11 million shares of Caterpillar at a market value of over $1.5 billion. Caterpillar is a member of Dow stock and specializes in making heavy machinery and equipment used for mining, energy, and agriculture. It possesses a market capitalization of $86.48 billion. Caterpillar was ranked 65th in 2017 on Fortune 500.

Waste Management

The fourth-largest company in the foundation's portfolio is Waste Management, Inc. The foundations hold more than 18.6 million shares at a market rate of $1.52 billion. Waste management is responsible for providing waste management and other environment associated services. It happens to be the largest waste management business in the country, with over 21 million customers. The company has a market capitalization of $39.55 billion and was ranked 202 in 2017 on Fortune 500.

Canadian National Railway Company

The fifth-largest company in the portfolio of the foundation is the Canadian National Railway Company. The foundation owns 17.1 million shares of the company at a market value of $1.4 billion. Canadian National Railway Company provides services related to integrated transportation such as freight forwarding, trucking, and warehousing. The company is mainly responsible for transporting petroleum products, fertilizers, coals, metals, and automotive products. The company has a market capitalization of $65 billion.

The purpose of mentioning the companies above was to observe and notice the fact that Bill Gates is interested in companies that have large market capitalization and have a strong grip in the markets where they operate. This provides Bill Gates an idea of how risky or fruitful investing in a company would be.

Warren Buffett

Warren Buffet, who is also known as "the Oracle of Omaha," believes in diversifying his portfolio. Even though he has comparatively fewer shares in the communication and consumer discretionary sector that does not draw him toward selling the stocks. As long as the company is moving towards growth, it will have Warren Buffet's attention.

He has famously said that even if he had a small investment, he could compound it to 50% in about a year's time. That is confidence and belief in his skills and knowledge of the industry. As a new investor, the best decision you can make is to follow the footsteps of those who have tread on the path before. And Warren Buffet's investment strategies are one for the folklores.

Buffet has pretty basic principles that he follows. And that perhaps is one of his strongest qualities - that no matter how the market is doing, he will follow his principles to yield higher returns in the long run. He believes people should only invest in companies that showcase 'sold fundamentals and potential for continuous growth.'

At the core of it, the concept is pretty basic, but what is difficult is its implementation in the real world. But if he can take $10,000 and turn it into a net worth over $86 billion, then there is little doubt that his strategies work. He has also managed to create a value of over $400 billion for his shareholders. Here is a look at his portfolio.

46.04% of his Portfolios consist of Financials

These include insurance companies and money center banks. He owns stakes in multiple companies, including Wells Fargo, Bank of America, JPMorgan Chase, US Bancorp, Moody's, Bank of NY Mellon, Goldman Sachs, Visa, Travelers, MasterCard, Synchrony Financial and Globe Life among others.

Over 25% of His Portfolio is invested in the Information Technology Sector

Maybe calling it the entire sector is a stretch. Buffet solely invests in Apple when it comes to technology. But he invests heavily! For every $4, more than $1 is invested or tied up with the technology giant.

15% of His investments are Tied Up in Consumer Staples

These have seen a dip in recent years. Berkshire Hathaway's investment in this sector has dipped down from over 45% to around a decade ago, to just 15% in current times. Currently, he owns shares in Kraft Heinz, Coca-Cola, Procter & Gamble, Costco, and Mondalez International. Coca-Cola takes up 10% of this consumer portfolio, where the remaining 5% is divided among other companies.

4.71% is invested in Transports

Going by his mantra to truly diversify one's portfolio, less than 5% is invested in transport, mainly airlines.

Buffet entered this sector during the middle of the last decade, in 2016, and there are speculations that his investments in this sector will likely increase in the near future. These investments include Delta Airlines, American Airlines Group, Unite Airlines Group, and UPS.

His decision to invest in airlines in specific has met with a lot of confusion and debate because amongst all his other investments; this one seems to be a bit on the riskier side. Airlines have a track record of not being able to survive economic downturns, but again, one can muse over his investment decisions, but one knows better than to question them. One reasoning could be the plunging prices of crude oil, which have made airlines quite profitable in recent years.

And Others

The remaining less than 10% has been invested in a variety of sectors, including communications, real estate, materials, healthcare, consumer discretionary, and energy. The companies include VeriSign, Charter Communications, Phillips 66, Occidental Petroleum, and Johnson & Johnson, among many others.

The dividend investment growth portfolio of Warren Buffet.

Ticker	Name	Sector	Industry	Dividend Yield	Dividend Safety
AAL	American Airlines Group	Industrials	Airlines	1.49	33
AXP	American Express Company	Financials	Consumer Finance	1.3	80
AAPL	Apple	Information Technology	Technology Hardware, Storage and Peripherals	0.97	99
BAC	Bank of America Corporation	Financials	Diversified Banks	2.17	89
BK	Bank of New York Mellon Corporation	Financials	Asset Management and Custody Banks	2.76	73
KO	Coca-Cola Company	Consumer Staples	Soft Drinks	2.81	80
COST	Costco Wholesale Corporation	Consumer Staples	Hypermarkets and Super Centers	0.84	99
DAL	Delta Air Lines	Industrials	Airlines	2.8	61
GM	General Motors Company	Consumer Discretionary	Automobile Manufacturers	4.52	61
GL	Globe Life	Financials	Life and Health Insurance	0.66	92
GS	Goldman Sachs Group	Financials	Investment Banking and Brokerage	2.06	91
JNJ	Johnson & Johnson	Healthcare	Pharmaceuticals	2.54	99
JPM	JPMorgan Chase & Co.	Financials	Diversified Banks	2.68	79
KHC	Kraft Heinz Company	Consumer Staples	Packaged Foods and Meats	5.31	29

MA	Mastercard Incorporated	Information Technology	Data Processing and Outsourced Services	0.5	99
MDLZ	Mondelez International	Consumer Staples	Packaged Foods and Meats	2.08	66
MCO	Moody's Corporation	Financials	Financial Exchanges and Data	0.77	83
MTB	M&T Bank Corporation	Financials	Regional Banks	2.58	99
OXY	Occidental Petroleum Corporation	Energy	Integrated Oil and Gas	7.67	50
PSX	Phillips 66	Energy	Oil and Gas Refining and Marketing	3.72	65
PNC	PNC Financial Services Group	Financials	Regional Banks	3.07	82
PG	Procter & Gamble Company	Consumer Staples	Household Products	2.37	99
QSR	Restaurant Brands International	Consumer Discretionary	Restaurants	3.19	62
SIRI	Sirius XM Holdings	Communications	Cable and Satellite	0.75	61
LUV	Southwest Airlines Co.	Industrials	Airlines	1.25	99
STOR	STORE Capital Corporation	Real Estate	Diversified REITs	3.59	61
SU	Suncor Energy	Energy	Integrated Oil and Gas	4.02	71
SYF	Synchrony Financial	Financials	Consumer Finance	2.7	53

CONCLUSION

The challenging times and ever-changing business landscape are encouraging many people to seek out various income-generating options. Retirees are often faced with various options to choose from in order to invest their savings, maximize rewards while minimizing the risks associated with their investments. With various investment options available in the market, the dividend investment strategy seems to be a safer and more stable investment option

Dividend investments can help individuals prepare for retirement, create exponential wealth, and make smarter financial decisions for themselves and their families. However, all this requires in-depth research and more than just monetary investment. This book can only offer guidance, but its implementation is up to you.

It is quite easy to gain information and study successful investors, but the application is the difficult part. While knowledge about the subject can influence decision making, it can be difficult to make the right decisions in the heat of the moment when your money is on the line.

A good idea would be to create a system and stick to the system, no matter how simple or complex it seems. Does it mean you should be carrying weights of dead horses or dead investments? Of course not! It just means don't make impulsive decisions but rather wait for markets to stabilize and offer the returns it promised!

You also need to keep your goals at the forefront. Your investments require a path, a destination in order to organically grow in the right direction. I hope this book has helped you find your path to tread on with your investments. All the best and good luck!

www.ingramcontent.com/pod-product-compliance
Lightning Source LLC
Chambersburg PA
CBHW071414210326
41597CB00020B/3503